W9-DAJ-896

Other Kaplan Books That Can Help with Reality

The Buck Starts Here
Going Indie: Self-Employment, Freelance, & Temping Opportunities
Résumé Builder & Career Counselor
Kaplan Guide to Distance Learning
Student's Guide to On-Campus Job Recruitment
Yale Daily News Working Knowledge
Careers in Communications and Entertainment
Careers in Nursing
John Douglas's Guide to Careers in the FBI
John Douglas's Guide to the Police Officer Exams

In Case You Decide to Delay Reality . . .

Graduate School Admissions Adviser
Law School Admissions Adviser
Medical School Admissions Adviser
Yale Daily News Guide to Fellowships and Grants

REALITY 101

Second Edition

by Fran Katzanek

Simon & Schuster

SYDNEY • LONDON • SINGAPORE • NEW YORK • TORONTO

Kaplan Books
Published by Simon & Schuster
1230 Avenue of the Americas
New York, NY 10020

For bulk sales to schools, colleges, and universities, please contact Renee Memi, Simon & Schuster Special Markets, 1633 Broadway, 8th Floor, New York, NY 10019.

Kaplan® is a registered trademark of Kaplan Educational Centers.

Project Editor: Eileen Mager
Online Research: Lori DeGeorge
Cover Design: Cheung Tai
Production Editor: Maude Spekes
Desktop Publishing Manager: Michael Shevlin
Managing Editor: David Chipps
Executive Editor: Del Franz

Special thanks to: Richard Christiano, Gerard Capistrano, and Evelyn Lontok

Manufactured in the United States of America
Published simultaneously in Canada

May 2000

10 9 8 7 6 5 4 3 2 1

Library of Congress Cataloging-in-Publication Data is available.

ISBN: 0-684-87330-3

CONTENTS

ABOUT THE AUTHOR

Fran Katzanek was Director of Career Services at Roger Williams University in Bristol, Rhode Island, for 15 years. At Roger Williams, she and her staff assisted thousands of students in the evaluation of their personal and career goals, conducting innovative workshops, teaching seminars, and delivering presentations to organizations and schools. This book is based upon her popular and successful "Reality 101" seminar for graduating seniors.

Katzanek's other career as a parent has allowed her to live on both sides of the proverbial fence: One son returned home right after college and stayed for several years. Another son "stopped out" twice before returning to college and graduating with honors. Her daughter returned home eight years after graduating to search for a new, more exciting career path. The search took almost three years, but she found it!

This book is dedicated to my two families: My children, Andy, Jay, Sheryl, Jen, and Brenda; and the wonderful family of students from whom I have learned so much.

INTRODUCTION

During my 15 years as Director of Career Services at Roger Williams University I learned that the two most panic-provoking questions I could ask a college senior are, "What are you going to do after graduation?" and "Do you know where you'll be on June 30, a month after you've left college?"

I learned that those two questions usually evoked the same startled expression on the student's face: A look of sheer panic, which included smiling lips over clenched teeth, raised eyebrows, and a heightened color to the cheeks—usually, deep red. Why? Why were seniors who were about to embark on an exciting adventure not excited by the prospect of graduating and pursuing a career for which they had spent a considerable amount of time preparing? What caused them to become immobilized and revert to a state of total denial about their imminent departure from the campus?

At the same time each year, I became increasingly aware of a general avoidance of the Career Services office after the students returned from their winter break. Members of the senior class would chat with me and share stories and jokes if l happened to bump into them in the student union or cafeteria, but I noticed a definite slowdown of scheduled appointments to my office as graduation drew near. At a time when members of the senior class should have been caught up in the excitement of making plans for the next portion of their lives, they showed a decided lack of energy and enthusiasm.

As I investigated this phenomenon, I learned that my colleagues at other colleges were noticing similar patterns of behavior in their senior students. While we in Career Services were seeing just a fraction of the senior class, the staff at the college's Counseling Center was being inundated with students seeking appointments for personal counseling. People seemed to be more irritable. The number of alcohol-related incidents on campus increased. Clearly, the issues the students were most concerned with went beyond finding that first job. Was it possible that this inertia they were experiencing was related to the process of making the transition from college to the real world? Were these fears and uncertainties at the core of their unusual behavior?

After talking with a good many seniors it became clear to me that there were two distinct aspects to the problem. The first, and possibly the more intense was fear of the impending separation from the safe environment of the college. The other major cause of avoidance of any kind of planning was the students' imminent entry into a world of work about which they knew little. I learned that students became immobilized because they were gripped by an insecurity relating to the world outside the college walls. After all, this would be the first time in their lives that they would not be in school. Through the years, they'd been successful at studying and passing exams and now they would be without a prescribed curriculum for the first time in their lives. The rules for success in the world beyond the classroom were not the same . . . or were they? What, in fact, were the rules out there? Outside the safe environment of the college they would be faced with many choices for which there would be no right or wrong answers. Real life would not resemble a true-or-false exam for which they could study.

From my own experience, I've learned that apprehensions about the unknown in our lives often lead to procrastination, avoidance, and indecisiveness. Many of us find our own unique methods to put off completing those tasks that overwhelm us or that we really don't enjoy doing. Years ago, while teaching a freshman seminar course, we talked about the art of procrastination. Everyone shared their favorite method of goofing off with the class. One student enjoyed color-coding every blouse that hung in her closet, and worked at that, instead of balancing her checkbook each month. Another alphabetized his cassette and CD collections when he wanted to avoid starting major projects for his American history class. I have a pile of mail order catalogues that I save, pull out, and reexamine whenever I want to avoid completing a task that I dislike doing. I call it "creative avoidance."

It occurred to me that we, at Career Services, desperately needed to address the behaviors exhibited by members of the senior class. We needed to examine the issues they were *really* concerned about, and we needed to talk about and deal with the specific fears that were plaguing them. Finding that first job was only part of the problem: Clearly there were a good many other factors that were more pressing and needed to be addressed. I became convinced that these "secondary" concerns, once brought out into the open and discussed, would somehow free the seniors and allow them to tackle those issues which would help them make a successful transition to the next phase of their lives.

These questions surfaced most frequently in my informal talks with students:

"What kind of work do I really want to do?"
"How will I ever find an apartment in an unfamiliar city?"
"What if I have to move back home with my parents?"
"How will I be able to learn to live on a tight budget?"

After carefully observing the symptoms of "senioritis," I became aware of the dire need to set aside some time each week to talk with graduating seniors. In addition to talking, we also needed to listen to their concerns. Perhaps an ongoing dialogue would give the students enough confidence to at least start making plans for the next phase of their lives. How could we make the process of exploration both meaningful and enjoyable?

A group of 10 students and I met for several weeks to talk about the major issues involved in making the transition from college to the world of work. Our weekly get-togethers were held at a house near campus, rented by four of the seniors in the pilot group. As we dined on pizza and soda supplied by Career Services, we talked about all of the aspects of leaving college that members of the group were concerned with. Absolutely no subjects were off-limits.

Each session started with casual conversation, which sometimes included responses to campus events, occurrences in our personal lives, or perhaps reactions to an international event. Gradually, the conversation drifted towards the impending reality of leaving the proscribed life the seniors were currently experiencing and entering the unknown world of work. The questions, "What are you most apprehensive about?" and "What scares you the most?" usually opened the floodgates and evoked honest, uninhibited responses. We soon discovered that leaving friends behind and becoming a valued member of the workplace ranked high on everybody's list of apprehensions. At one session, the conversation drifted towards finding good medical facilities in a new city. When one of the seniors quietly announced that he was still seeing his pediatrician, several others smiled and confessed that they, too, were embarrassed each time they visited their pediatrician and noticed how much they towered over the younger patients in the waiting room.

The sessions provided much laughter. There were tears as well. Most important, there was dialogue. The more we talked, the more we discovered that our fears and apprehensions were not unique—they were shared by others. At our final meeting, we listed those apprehensions that appeared most frequently on everyone's list of major concerns and came up with the following:

- I don't know how to deal with pressure and calls from home inquiring about progress with résumés and interviews.

- I don't really know what's out there for people with my major.

- What if I hate the job I choose?

- What if I have to return home and live with my parents?

- Where will I live if I can't go home to my parents?

- What have I really learned in college? How capable am I?

- Will my employers know what my faults are?

- What will my co-workers be like? Will there be other employees my age?

- How will I make new friends? Will I ever see my college friends again?

Sound familiar? Are these the same issues you're dealing with? Welcome to the complex world facing college seniors everywhere. One great advantage you *do* have, which previous generations did not, is the accessibility of vast amounts of information at the click of a mouse. Throughout this book, you'll find sidebars describing ways in which the Internet can help you start your new life in the "real world." From job listings to apartment listings, medical directories to investment advice, these online resources can make your difficult transition a little bit easier.

Other sidebars offer a more personal perspective: I've included comments written by alumni who had participated in Reality 101 sessions when they were seniors. I've also asked several students still in college, as well as parents of recent graduates, to share their views and experiences. I believe we can all learn a great deal by listening to each other's voices.

Welcome to *Reality 101*!

starting your
NEW CAREER

chapter 1
EVERYONE ELSE'S EXPECTATIONS

"I have many thoughts as I sit here at my desk in what is to be my last dorm room. I also have many concerns and questions as the time between being an undergrad and a graduate shortens. I am worried, after having my exit-loan meeting, that I won't find a job by the time the bills start to come in. I am also worried that if I do find a job, I won't like it, won't be able to perform the associated tasks, or won't be able to support myself should I want to move out.

"Because I intend to move home with my parents, I worry that I'll miss the unencumbered freedom I have grown so accustomed to here at school. At this point I have more freedom than I've ever known, and I am not ready to sacrifice that by going home.

"Most of all, however, I will miss the many friends I made over the past five years! I am going to miss not seeing them every day, having meals together, and just visiting. I am about to leave a totally comfortable and somewhat laid-back environment to enter a chaotic and often unfriendly world of business. I know I can succeed; the question is just, 'When?'"
—S. Sarkisian, Class of '97

College seniors rarely discuss their postgraduation plans with classmates because each is convinced that no one else has doubts about where she's going and how she's going to get there. You may think that everyone else has a definite plan in place, but let me assure you that the person sitting next to you in your senior seminar class is probably beset by the same uncertainties and insecurities that you feel. It's all part of the process of stepping out from behind the safety of the college walls and into the world beyond.

Can you remember how you felt as you approached the campus on your first day as a college student four or five years ago? The situation was different, but the questions surrounding your uncertainties were probably very similar to those that are nagging at you now. Think back for a moment and try to recall your fears and what it felt like that first day at college.

Did your parents pressure you to do well and get high grades? Were you worried about your choice of major? If you had already declared a major, were you concerned that it wasn't going to be the right one for you? What if you had made the wrong choice? Were you uncertain about liking and getting along with your new roommate? Were you concerned about your ability to do college-level work? Perhaps you were thinking about the cafeteria and who you would sit with for dinner on that first day.

The scenario may have changed, but the questions and underlying fears are very much the same. Remember that you *have* succeeded in college. You *were* able to deal, successfully, with all the issues that seemed so frightening to you on that September day as you embarked on your career as a college student.

The next stage of your life is not all that different. You've worked hard and have learned a great deal. Sure, you may have failed some exams or perhaps even a course along the way, but you *have* succeeded in earning a college degree. Hopefully you've also learned how to cope, in a more positive way, with your fear of the unknown. If, at this point, you have no clue as to what you want to be when you grow up, that's all right. Now is as good a time as any to start exploring your options and make plans for embarking on another new and exciting adventure.

Marsha Sinetar, author of *Do What You Love and the Money Will Follow*, talks about the concept of "right livelihood," the process of consciously choosing the right kind of work for ourselves. She says, "Unfortunately, since we learn early to act on what others say, value, and expect, we often find ourselves a long way down the wrong road before

> "Leaving college is not stuff you talk about while hanging out in the dorms, but it's on everybody's mind."
>
> —S. Foley, Class of '96.

realizing we did not actually choose our work. Turning our lives around is usually the beginning of maturity since it means correcting choices made unconsciously, without deliberation or thought.

"The ability to choose our work is no small matter. It takes courage to act on what we value and to willingly accept the consequences of our choices. Being able to choose means not allowing fear to inhibit or control us, even though our choices may require us to act against our fears or against the wishes of those we love and admire. Choosing sometimes forces us to leave secure and familiar arrangements."

People choose to enter a specific field of work for various reasons, not all of them good. Sometimes parental pressure plays a part in your choice of a major. Sometimes the projected demands of the marketplace influence your choice. During my years as a career counselor I learned that the majority of us, when we enter college, really have no clear ideas about the many career options available to us. Most people choose majors arbitrarily and hope they've made the right choice.

Those few souls who are absolutely certain about their fields of study are usually people who have a special talent and are driven by a passion to utilize that talent. Most of the art, drama, and music majors I've spoken with have probably known what their college curriculum would be since the fifth grade. When I talk with students who are studying fine arts or architecture and ask at which point in their lives they had decided to enter a related career, the responses are always the same. Almost all of them indicate that they started to draw or perform as young children and knew, beyond a doubt, that they'd pursue a career using their special talent. I've always envied these innately gifted folks. The rest of us just don't have that kind of talent, and most of us lack the passion that drives these creative artists.

You've probably thought, from time to time, about some sort of work that really appeals to you. At one time or another you may have fantasized about a specific career you thought might be interesting and that you'd like to pursue. Still, you may not be able to come up with a special name or job title for the kind of work that really appeals to you. That's

"The thought of going out into the real world was extremely frightening, and I suppose that's why I wanted to postpone it as long as I could. I was scared because I knew that after graduation I had to find a job, and that alone was a lot of pressure. I also was not focused on what I really wanted to do and did not have a career path or a goal. I realized that for the first time in my life I would not be going to school in September, and this included not seeing friends and classmates with whom I had shared my life for four years. Finally, the thought of having to pay back thousands of dollars in student loans was the most frightening of all!"

—S. Kayata, Class of '92

okay because putting a label on your dream job doesn't really matter at this point. Giving yourself the freedom to get in touch with your likes and dislikes is what counts. Let's investigate your ideas while you allow yourself to really get in touch with your feelings. This is the time to suspend all "shoulds" and allow yourself to fantasize.

VISUALIZING YOUR IDEAL JOB

Take 10 minutes to relax in quiet surroundings and allow yourself to get in touch with your feelings about the career that is ideal for you: Forget all the advice you've received along the way from friends and relatives, and assume that education and experience are not important factors in the career that intrigues you. It might be a good idea to do this exercise with a friend, having one person read the script while the other tries to visualize her ideal situation.

Close your eyes. Imagine yourself getting ready for an ordinary day at work. What time do you wake up? Are you living in an apartment or a house? Do you have roommates? As you begin to dress, notice what type of clothes you will wear. Are you dressed casually, are you wearing a business suit? Perhaps you're in some sort of uniform. How do you get to work? Are you driving your car or taking the bus? Perhaps you see yourself driving to a train station and getting on a commuter train.

Now you arrive at work. What are your surroundings like? Are you in a spacious loft? Do you work at home or are you parking your car in a suburban industrial park? Are you in a city? Do you work on the twenty-seventh floor of a skyscraper or the second floor of a rented storefront?

Once inside, do you have your own office or is your desk one of many set off by partitions? Do you report to someone or do you have people reporting to you? What tasks are you performing? Are you organizing things? Are you on the phone a great deal of your work day? Do you have to move around a lot or are you mostly at your desk? Do clients come to see you? Do you travel to other cities? Do you go to multiple job sites? Do you work for a large company? How many employees work for the company: 10? 100? Thousands?

What are your lunch breaks like? Do you dine with clients in a fancy restaurant or do you eat with co-workers in the company cafeteria? Perhaps you imagine yourself eating by yourself at your desk.

It is now afternoon. Have you gone to any meetings today? Are you stressed out, or is your mood as stable as it was when you arrived this morning? Do you have to make schedules for tomorrow? Can you leave some of your work for completion tomorrow, or are you under a deadline? What time is it when you leave?

How do you feel when you arrive home: excited by your day's work or exhausted? Do you have enough time to read, watch your favorite program on television, or visit with friends? Or is it already time for bed?

All right, open your eyes. What did you learn about the kind of lifestyle you'd like in your ideal day? Were you surprised at some of your responses? Did you have trouble visualizing any part? Your lifestyle preferences are an important factor in taking the first step toward pursuing the career you really want.

"The uncertainty of the future was terrifying. I was afraid of failure—failing my family, my teachers, and especially myself! I also felt anxiety about living with my parents again. I felt sure I was in for a rough ride. Talking with other seniors made me aware of the fact that I wasn't the only person beset by fear, anxiety, and uncertainty. That helped a lot."

—M. Vieira, Class of '94

JOB HUNTING on the Web

The Internet has changed the dynamics of the employment marketplace. Never before have companies been able to present their job opportunities to the public so freely, and never before have job seekers been able to bring so much attention to their résumés. Some of the available information and search aids you can find on most job search sites include the following:

- Job listings, sorted by geographical area, occupation, salary, etcetera
- Résumé posting
- Company profiles (many with links to company homepages)
- Personal search agents who will e-mail you job openings that match your search criteria, as the openings are posted
- Chats and message boards to post your career questions and job hunting concerns
- Career management information
- Articles offering career-related advice and breaking news in various industries
- Career fair information and links
- Salary comparisons among different industries and locations
- Online shopping areas that sell career-related books and products

Comprehensive Career Sites

Most of the sites below contain either all or a combination of the resources listed above. Please note that these sites represent only a small fraction of the job search sites available to you. It would have been possible to fill an entire book with the pros, cons, and specifics of every career site on the Web, but we'll allow you to discover each site's quirks and nuances for yourself. To get you started, we've listed some standout features of some of the top career Web sites:

www.careerbuilder.com

One of the biggest career sites, it gathers listings for its "Mega Job Search" from more than 30 *other* major job search sites, allowing you to search thousands and thousands of listings by location, job type, keyword, pay range, etcetera.

www.monster.com

Hugely popular, this site is easy to navigate, has a lot of job openings (about 250,000 from more than 30,000 employers), and offers a great personal career management function called "My Monster" that allows you to manage your résumé, update your search criteria, and track your job applications.

www.vault.com
Another great site with lots of job listings (approximately 200,000 jobs posted by 21,000 employers), great resources, and a really extensive message board.

www.headhunter.net
Headhunter charges companies for ad placement based on how and where they'd like an ad to appear during a job search (a boldfaced ad with a border that comes up first in a job search is much more expensive than an ad with regular type that pops up last). Fortunately for you, you can also affect the placement of your e-résumé in a company's search for employees by upgrading your position for a small fee of $10, $20, or $30.

www.careersite.com
Although other sites will also keep your search information confidential, this site it particularly careful about blocking your name, contact information, and current employer.

www.hotjobs.com
This site is similar to Monster.com in its broad scope of listings and its very attractive personal search management function called "My Hot Jobs" (I wonder who copied whom, huh?). What is particularly impressive about this site is its amazing company profile collection. By clicking on a particular company logo, you can access all the job openings in that company.

www.careermosaic.com
With all the amenities of most other job-search sites, this one also has a great subsection called the "College Connection," with advice and resources compiled specifically for college seniors and recent graduates. In addition, the "College Connection" has a list of links that can help you in all aspects of your job search.

www.jobtrak.com
To access the job listings in this site, you must be a student or alumnus of a participating university; depending on your school, you may even need a password to enter. However, locks and keys aside, the jobs you find on this site are tailored for people of your age group and experience level.

www.thepavement.com
This career site for young adults (ages 20–26) focuses on the transition from college to professional life. It offers a national database of early-career job opportunities, tools to help you manage your budget, and numerous articles giving practical advice on career-related issues.

Classifieds Online

Your days of purchasing the 20-pound edition of the Sunday paper are over! Instead, grab your mouse to cruise the classifieds. The two sites below chose a different strategy in collecting their job listings. Their databases of jobs are compiled from the classified sections of respected newspapers across the country.

www.classifiedventures.com   **www.careerpath.com**

Niche Sites

Niche job search sites are becoming more and more prevalent as the Internet expands and the huge sites become too cumbersome and intimidating for those who know exactly what they're looking for. It's no surprise that the computer technology field has led the pack with successful Web sites such as these:

www.dice.com   **www.techies.com**   **www.techjobbank.com**

A few other non-techie specialty sites:

www.interec.net
For all kinds of engineers.

www.guidestar.org
Searchable database of more than 60,000 nonprofit organizations.

www.writerswrite.com
Writing jobs in all areas: journalism, editorial, staff writers, freelance, technical writing, etcetera.

www.coolworks.com
Their tag line says it all: "Live and work where others only get to visit."

If you saw yourself arriving at your place of work in a car and dashing up the stairs of an ivy-covered, two-story brownstone to your office, you probably would not be very happy if your job required you to take a crowded train into New York City where you are squeezed into an elevator before exiting on the thirty-fifth floor of a skyscraper. If you pictured yourself dressed in casual clothes as you left for work in the morning, then being employed in the corporate headquarters of a large insurance company with a more formal dress code would probably not be your workplace of choice. We all have specific ideas about our ideal jobs. But at the same time, we need to be aware that there will always be concessions we'll have to make. At this point, why not go for it—take a chance and pursue your ideal job! After all, what's the worst thing that could happen?

Now let's turn your visualization exercise into a list of priorities that you have chosen for this first job. Let's suppose that you've discovered that you:

- Enjoy wearing business clothes every day.
- Prefer to interact with many people during your day at work.
- Look forward to commuting to and from work by train.
- Visualize your office or lab on the twentieth floor of a skyscraper.
- See yourself utilizing your good communication and problem-solving skills in your work.
- Really enjoy the pressure of a full workload.

After identifying your priorities, the next step is to identify where your preferences will fit in the world of work.

Before we continue, however, there are a few more questions you should consider. Take as much time as you need to come up with honest responses because your answers will help you zero in on values that are truly important to you. What activities make you feel energized, as if you've really made a difference? When in your life have you felt a tremendous amount of satisfaction from having completed a job? Why was it so satisfying? What things have you done in the past that have made you feel really good about yourself? Here's an interesting question: Is there a job that you believe is so interesting and exciting that you would work without being paid?

Now that you've given some serious thought to your work values, how do you plug these newly discovered priorities into your choice of a career? Notice we haven't put a label or job title on any specific career you should pursue. The priorities you've chosen could be met by working in anyone of a number of positions. You could possibly work in a hospital as a patient care representative, in an insurance company as an underwriter, as an assistant in the human resources department of a large corporation, or as a paralegal in a law firm. There are probably a dozen other career tracks you could follow which would satisfy your priorities as you begin this first venture into the working world.

Remember, it's *your* interests, *your* skills, and *your* abilities that will get you hired, and not the subject you happened to major in. A philosophy major whose priorities match those you've chosen could step into any of the career paths listed above. A person graduating with a degree in business, dance, or communications would do equally well if her skills, abilities, and priorities were similar to those mentioned.

Don't be concerned that your degree is in the wrong discipline for whatever job interests you. Of course, you won't be able to work in a chemistry lab or draw technical blueprints if you majored in psychology. There are, however, hundreds of nontechnical careers you might consider.

Employers look for people who have developed specific skills that are necessary in today's rapidly changing world. They are more interested in candidates' internship or summer work experience and their ability to learn new skills quickly than in their college majors. Give yourself permission to take a chance, to stretch your imagination, and really try to identify and pursue your fantasy career.

I found an interesting article in *Cosmopolitan* magazine (fall, winter 1996), that included a list of famous people, their current careers, and their college majors. Here are some of the unlikely pairings:

Paul Reiser, creator and costar of the former NBC series *Mad About You*, majored in music.

Phil Jackson, NBA coach, had triple majors: philosophy, psychology, and religion.

Lisa Kudrow, actress on NBC's *Friends*, majored in biology.

Lyle Lovett, country music star, majored in journalism.

Bill Watterson, creator of the *Calvin & Hobbes* comic strip, was a political science major.

Interesting, isn't it? In fact, a great many people work in fields that are not at all related to their college major. In order to be truly happy and challenged in our work, it's necessary to utilize our unique skills and abilities in our jobs.

Another way to get in touch with your talents is to identify those leisure activities you really enjoy. What do you find yourself doing when you have some free time? What do you do when you don't *have* to do anything? What skills do you use in these activities? Do you enjoy being with friends, or would you rather participate in a quiet activity by yourself? Do you collect stamps or coins? Do you enjoy building model airplanes, or would you rather go shopping?

Try to identify those skills you use in these leisure activities. For example, someone who can spend hours working on his coin collection, would probably enjoy working in a career that requires a great deal of attention to detail and not too much contact with large numbers of people. On the other hand, the person who is easily distracted when she hears voices outside of her dorm room, and who spends a good deal of her leisure time socializing and just hanging out, would not be very happy spending the greater part of her work day in an isolated area without frequent interaction with other people.

The trick is to identify your skills and then make sure the work you choose will utilize and demand those skills. For example, I love the challenges presented by solving all sorts of problems. I also enjoy being with people and doing presentations to groups. Career counseling enables me to utilize my

"As your senior year winds down and graduation quickly approaches, most individuals feel that they are not ready to leave: They get scared about not getting a good job, not being qualified enough, and not having what it takes to be successful. In college, if you received a bad grade on a test, or did poorly on an assignment, there was always the chance to study harder and bring your grade up. My fear was that, if I did poorly in life, I would never get the same opportunity again."

—G. Maggiolino, Class of '94

"I was eager to start working, then I realized that I've been working hard for four years. I needed a break to relax and figure out what I really wanted to do with myself. I'd advise new graduates not to get stressed out. It's easier said than done, but I realized that 90 percent of what's valuable to me in the real world, I learned outside the classroom, and will stay with me a lot longer than the careers or jobs I will have through the years. It all works out in the end."

—S. Foley, Class of '96

14

skills and has been a wonderful career for me. In college, I majored in English.

EXPLORING OPTIONS

If you're still not sure about what kind of work you'd like to do after giving serious thought to which direction you'd like to take, how about exploring other options? Some of you may have had difficulty visualizing your entry into the workforce. If you really aren't ready to choose and commit to a career path, you might like to consider taking a year off. Time off will help you focus on your career goals, allow you to gain valuable skills at the same time. A year off can also provide exciting experiences. Besides, you may never have the chance to take time off again!

There are literally hundreds of opportunities available that will give you an opportunity to gain experience, discover your skills, and learn about the world of work at the same time. Your college's career center is a good place to start researching options available to you. The reference librarian in your city or town can also help you locate organizations that are looking for the kind of help you are willing to give.

Employers agree that good communication skills and the ability to present ideas and converse are the most important traits they look for when hiring someone. The ability to think analytically and to research and write well also enhance a candidate's chances for employment. It is important, therefore, for you to make sure that your time off is spent improving those skills that will make you more marketable when you are ready to go job hunting. Try to choose a situation that will enable you to learn more about yourself at the same time.

VOLUNTEER OPPORTUNITIES on the Web

Want to "get involved" but have no idea how to start? The Internet will help you wade through thousands of potential volunteer opportunities in you area, narrowing down your search to the area and field of volunteerism in which you're most interested. The following Web sites offer a vast array of volunteer opportunities from which to choose:

www.GetInvolved.com (from the Community Action Network)

www.VolunteerMatch.com

www.Servenet.org

www.whitehouse.gov/WH/EOP/cns/html/amer/html
(the official site for AmeriCorps, a national service organization)

If you know the exact organization for which you'd like to volunteer your time and services, be sure to check its Web site for information on your local chapter. Since volunteers are always needed, contact information should be one of the first links you come across on the site.

If you didn't take advantage of any experiential learning opportunities such as internships or cooperative education assignments during your student days, be assured that it's not too late to gain valuable experience after graduation. There are a number of ways you can find opportunities that will enable you to acquire those skills you'll need in order to be competitive in the workplace. Some of the most effective ways are discussed in the following pages of this chapter. At the same time, you will have a chance to test market your ideal job and discover whether or not you'd like to pursue a specific career.

VOLUNTEERING

Volunteering is a great way to gain experience and assess your interest in a specific area of work at the same time. There are literally thousands of opportunities out there, and you will have to do some research and zero in on those that can help you gain career focus while you perform a valuable service. In the midst of the current national campaign to promote volunteerism, it should not be difficult to find a great many resources that

"Reality 101 helped me realize that starting at the bottom and working up is okay for a person right after college. My field of work is very competitive, and I realized that just getting an interview and a part-time job was an accomplishment. Not everyone will be offered the perfect job right out of college."

"The summer after I graduated, I moved back home to New Jersey, and got a part-time job as an instructor at the Aquarium for Wildlife Conservation in Brooklyn, New York. I truly love it, and I'm hoping a full-time position will be available soon."

—K. Deckert, Class of '96

will help you locate those opportunities that are right for you.

It's a good idea to start talking to your friends and faculty at school sometime during your senior year in order to identify possible volunteer work sites for you. Family members, too, can be very helpful when you're starting to network. Making a list of those organizations that offer the kinds of work situations that will enable you to gain experience and observe the day-to-day happenings in that workplace at the same time. Make a list of the kinds of experience you would like to have, ideally, as a volunteer. Keep in mind, too, some of the work and lifestyle values you chose in the visualization exercise. In order for the volunteer experience to be helpful, you must keep focusing on your needs and expectations.

Try to get names of people who currently work, or have worked, in organizations that are of interest to you. If you've decided City Hospital is where you'd like to volunteer, you could ask some neighbors, your cousins, the people whose lawn you cut years ago—everyone you can think of—for help with identifying connections. It's called networking! Your first step could be to get some background about City Hospital and about the kinds of volunteer opportunities available there. It's important to keep a record of people you've talked with, in case you might need to contact them at a later date. It's also a good idea to send a short note thanking them for the time they spent with you.

Hospitals offer a great many opportunities for career exploration. Writing newsletters, assisting with research projects, or helping to solve patient's concerns about their bills are just a few of the areas you might consider working in as a volunteer. If you think you'd like to pursue a career in medical illustration, the media center of a hospital could offer valuable experience to you. Performing a variety of duties as a volunteer is a great way to build your résumé.

It will be necessary for you to make an appointment to meet with the coordinator of volunteers in order to discuss specific volunteer opportu-

SOME VOLUNTEER ORGANIZATIONS	TYPE OF EXPERIENCE
American Diabetes Association (www.diabetes.org)	Medical
Chambers of Commerce (www.chambers-of-commerce.com)	Business, communications
Visiting Nurses (www.vna.org)	Medical, business
Child & Family Services	Advocacy
American Heart Association (www.americanheart.org)	Communications, medical
Special Olympics	Special advocacy
Volunteers for Educational & Social Services (VESS)	Social services, counseling, business
Regional zoos	Science, communications, planning
Community food banks	Advocacy, social services
Animal rescue shelters	Public relations, biology, communications
Senior citizens centers	Social services, recreation, advocacy
Literacy centers	Education, social services
Habitat for Humanity (www.habitat.org)	Construction, planning
Family AIDS centers	Social services, medical, communications
Local correctional facilities	Social services, education, recreation
Local 4-H Associations (www.4h-usa.org)	Science, education, advocacy

"Life does take funny and strange turns. I'm now living in Hawaii! I moved out here in January and am planning on staying until the summer. I'm only waitressing, but I'm having a blast. When I move home this summer, I plan to apply for a job teaching autistic children. I'm really excited that things are going so well!"

—S. Foley, Class of '96

nities available for a person with your skills. It's always a good idea to let this person know what your strengths are, and to find out where in the hospital organization a person with your talents could be utilized and challenged. Perhaps you will have an opportunity to help design your ideal job as a volunteer. It really is possible!

If you think you might like to teach, how about volunteering at a Head Start program? Would you enjoy working with teenagers in an inner-city setting? There are many federal, state, and local programs to investigate. Schools for the hearing-impaired and other special-needs populations often welcome interns as well. Teaching English abroad can be a rewarding experience that gives you the opportunity to learn about other cultures firsthand. Living in another country and climate offers a chance to gain effective communication skills while you learn to work with diverse populations. Museums, too, offer lots of opportunities for people who would like to test their interest in teaching. Whether you work as a tour guide in an art museum or explain marine and animal habits to small groups of children in an aquarium or zoo, you will be able to see firsthand what being with groups of children and teaching is like.

If you're interested in history, you could do research or work with an archivist in a corporate setting or possibly in a nonprofit organization. Many cities and towns have historical societies where assistance with organizing and promoting events is very much in demand and appreciated.

There are literally hundreds of opportunities for you to gain hands-on experience. Some options you might want to explore include City Year (www.city-year.org), an organization modeled on the Peace Corps but located in primarily urban areas. Habitat for Humanity International (www.habitat.org), based in Americus, Georgia, provides an opportunity to build and restore dwellings, while working with people from other parts of the country. Teaching English in the Czech Republic or other eastern European countries, doing research in a rainforest, or becoming involved in environmental activism are just a few of the many adventurous options you might like to pursue. *Transitions Abroad* is a bimonthly magazine that offers a wealth of information about economical, purposeful, international travel and work opportunities. Your college library or career center will probably have copies of this interesting and helpful magazine, or you can access it online at www.transabroad.com.

> "When I left college, I began working on a cruise ship. I'm happy I made that decision because it made me appreciate the fact that I had a college degree. Although I met a lot of nice people, visited interesting places, and had some great experiences, the work was very hard, and I left in the fall."
>
> —S. Kayata, Class of '92

Additionally, Big Brothers/Big Sisters of America (www.bbsa.org), City Cares of America (cares.org/national), Literacy Volunteers of America (www.literacyvolunteers.org), and the Points of Light Foundation (www.pointsoflight.org) are just a few of the many social service organizations that can refer you to volunteer opportunities in your area. Visit their Web sites to learn more about these organizations. A reference librarian can also be very helpful in assisting you with your search for organizations looking for volunteers who have specialized skills.

This is your chance to dream big and go for it! Not only will volunteering help build a better society, it will build your résumé and enable you to get good references if you put forth your best efforts. Because of an increasing national emphasis on volunteerism, more and more employers look favorably upon the concept of deferring your job search and spending time helping others.

SHADOWING

You may choose to work in a variety of non-career related jobs while you search for your ideal field of work. Working as a salesperson, waitress, or clerk will enable you to make some money while your career explo-

19

ration continues. If you choose to take this route, you should plan to spend some of your free time *shadowing*, which is the concept of following or spending time with someone in his place of work. Shadowing will give you an opportunity to communicate and network with people in the workforce who can help inform you about the realities of specific careers. You will need to be creative in order to identify people who are working in what you believe is your ideal job. It might be a friend's cousin, a neighbor, or a relative you haven't seen for a while.

Perhaps you could have another brainstorming session with your friends and family and try to create a list of people who have the kind of job you think you'd like to pursue. If you can't come up with any names, you might consider contacting the alumni office at your college. They may have a list of people who work in various disciplines and have volunteered to meet with students. Most colleges have some form of shadowing program that allows students to spend time observing a variety of workplaces. At Roger Williams University, the Career Services office maintained a list of alumni who agreed to participate in the program,

SALARY INFO on the Web

There's no denying it: Salary is often the deciding factor in choosing a job. But how do you know what you're worth? The links and resources on these sites will help you come up with a reasonable, competitive salary for the positions you are considering.

www.erieri.com
The Economic Research Institute's Web site contains salary surveys; calculators adjust for living costs in different areas or cities.

www.acinet.org
America's Career InfoNet site provides salaries for the same job in five or more cities.

www.bls.gov
The Bureau of Labor Statistics contains the most comprehensive collection of Web-based salary data.

www.jobstar.org
For the salary-obsessed job seeker, this site provides links to over 300 salary surveys.

and help students explore their options. After all, most alumni remember going through the same doubts and uncertainties you are experiencing now when they were undergraduates.

Shadowing can take place for one day, for a week, or even for a longer period of time. Some alums invite the student to lunch, explain the day-to-day responsibilities of their jobs, and invite the student to spend a specified amount of time with them in their place of business. It's a great way to find out if you'd like to continue investigating and exploring your ideal work situation.

INFORMATIONAL INTERVIEWS

After you've identified the people you'd like to shadow, you will have to phone them or write a business letter explaining that you are interested in exploring the kind of work they are currently engaged in and would like information about the nature of their daily tasks. State that you will call in a week to see if an appointment is possible.

If spending time at the workplace is not possible, perhaps you could request an informational interview, which at least will give you a chance to speak with a professional in your field of interest. Be clear that you are seeking career information, not job offers. *Do not use shadowing or informational interview time to ask for a job!*

Here's a sample of appropriate questions you might ask of someone whom you are shadowing or talking with at an informational interview:

- How did you get started in this type of work?
- What do you like most about your work? What don't you like?
- What skills are required for this kind of work?
- What do you find most rewarding?
- What do you do in a typical day?
- Would you advise young people to enter this career area? Why or why not?
- What, in your opinion, is the job outlook in this field? What will affect its growth or decline?

- What are some related positions a person interested in this area might explore?
- Who else do you know whom I might talk with? May I use your name when I contact this person?

Always dress professionally when you visit the workplace, and it's a good idea to have several copies of your résumé with you, just in case (but don't take them out unless asked). After you've conducted this informational type interview, don't forget to write a brief thank-you note soon after your meeting. I know a good many people who were contacted several months after their informational interview took place and informed of current openings in the company. The impression you make today may help you get a job in the future.

You're probably wondering how you're going to do all this exploration and put bread on your table at the same time. We'll talk about that later. We'll also talk about dealing with the ever-present parental pressures to get started on a specific career track. For now, let's summarize. Hopefully, at this point, you will:

- Be aware of what lifestyle you think you'd like to pursue.
- Know which of your skills you'd like to utilize at work.
- Be prepared to plan, creatively, ways to gain experience as well as information about your chosen field.

Now let 's get ready to create a road map for your trip. One of the books in my career library is David P. Campbell's *If You Don't Know Where You're Going, You'll Probably End Up Somewhere Else*. I absolutely agree with that statement, so let's devise a plan that will help steer you in the right direction.

chapter 2
READY, SET, GOAL

"I think the best advice I have to give seniors is, first of all, to not be afraid of taking chances. You can always get a job waiting tables! So many of my college friends returned back home after graduation because they were afraid to go so far away or were afraid they might not make it. The truth is, you'll never know unless you try. I know that has become somewhat of a cliché over the years, but it is the truth. Broaden your horizons; see yourself in a new city or in a new country. Try something new, and if you don't like it, you can always try something else. Don't think of it as a failure if your original plans don't work out—think of it as a career change.

"Secondly, have an idea of what you really want in a job before you go looking. Are you the kind of person who can do 'the nine-to-five,' or do you prefer a more flexible schedule? When you find it, stay there. Time does wonderful things for your experience level, your résumé, and, of course, your paycheck!"

—R. J. Polca, Class of '94

What steps do you need to take in order to reach your destination? How do you get started on your plan?

You've probably set some goals during your college career, so think of this exercise as a short review. Essentially, you need to know the difference between long- and short-term goals. Long-term goals usually focus on where you'd like to be a number of years from now. In your visualization exercise, you may have seen yourself as an administrator of a world-renowned hospital. You may have visualized your well-furnished office with a large desk near the window that overlooks the financial district of your city. On your desk is your nameplate, with the word *Director* written under your name.

Your long-term goal, then, is to make that visualization become a reality. But where to start? That's where short-term goals enter the picture. Setting and reaching a number of short-term goals are the steps you will need to take in order to make that visualization really happen. You may be aware that there are specific rules you should follow when you set a goal. If not, let's review.

- Choose a measurable goal and write it down. Be specific about what you want to achieve and by what date. *To be employed by next fall* is not specific enough and cannot be measured. *To be working as a volunteer in either County or City Hospital, and to have conducted two informational interviews by September 15* is very specific, and it is measurable.

- Determine whether the goal is achievable. If you've set this goal in April, will you have enough time to contact the hospitals, meet with the volunteer coordinators, and start your volunteer job by the date you've designated? If you're planning to take a few weeks or a month off after graduation, will you have enough time to contact those alumni you'd like to shadow? You may have to modify the goal slightly in order to make it achievable.

- Make sure the goal is realistic. Are you aiming too high? Too low? At the same time, be sure that the goal is consistent with your skills and abilities and your values too. Can you identify why this goal is worthwhile for you? Does it fit in with your ideal lifestyle?

- Identify potential problems you might encounter in pursuing your goal. You may want to share your plan with a friend or relative who will be able to identify possible difficulties that you did not anticipate. Your friend might also be helpful in pointing out a solution to your problem. Sometimes two heads are better than one!

- Create specific strategies for achieving the goal. It sometimes helps to work backwards and create a time line. If September 15 is your target date, what steps need to be completed before then, and by what dates?

- Is your time line realistic and feasible?

At this point you might want to list the tools you will need in order to put your plan into action. Do you have a completed résumé and a list of alumni whom you'd like to contact? Do you have their current addresses? Have you made a list of those organizations you are interested in contacting? Have you written down your personal learning objectives? What would you like to get out of this experience? Do you have listed in a notebook the names and phone numbers of volunteer coordinators and other professionals you'd like to contact?

It's a good idea to keep a weekly log of your progress in finding your ideal work or volunteer situation. Use a notebook set aside specifically for your job/volunteer search. Write everything down: names of people you've contacted, dates you called or met with them—everything. If you've been a poor record keeper in the past, now is the time to begin changing your habits.

After you've started working, it's a good idea to keep a log of what you do and what you've learned to do. Which aspects of the day-to-day duties do you like? What elements of your work do you really dislike? What knowledge have you gained? What do you know now that you weren't aware of a month ago? Are the people who work in this area compatible with your interests and your values? Jotting down names of people you've gotten to know at work is also a good idea. They may become your reference and contact network sometime in the future.

"I would definitely advise senior students to network. Begin with friends and family and find out what's out there for you. Most important, do not get discouraged. You will find the right match soon enough."

—A. Bearse, Class of '92

Remember, no matter how daring your ideal career idea may be, you *can* develop a plan that will move you in the right direction. *You* can make it happen!

FINDING TEMPORARY JOBS WHILE YOU'RE FINDING YOURSELF

So how are you going to support yourself while you gain experience and explore careers that interest you? And how are you going to explain your search to your parents? What kinds of summer jobs have you had in the past? Very often, your summer employer will agree to allow you flexibility in your work schedule if you explain your career exploration plan. If that's not a possibility, are there other, similar businesses that you could contact? What skills did you gain in your summer job? Where could these skills be utilized? Even if the only summer job you've had was being a lifeguard, your experience working with people of all ages, your good problem-solving skills, and your ability to communicate well will help you gain employment elsewhere.

If you've had experience waiting tables, make a list of all the better eating places in town and start applying for jobs at these restaurants. Working as a waiter offers flexibility in terms of time, a fairly decent salary, and also the opportunity to meet people and network.

I'm always amazed at how many graduates who take this route are able to get interviews and jobs as a result of chatting with the customers they serve. Most people have either been in your situation or know of someone who has, and they are really willing to help others get started.

"Most of my classmates had no job prospects, and when May's commencement ceremony rolled around they were packing it up to move in with Mom and Dad. I didn't have that option, so I was sending résumés out long before graduation. What I feared most was having to put more pressure on my mother, because I knew that she could not take on my financial burden. With my student loans, credit card debt from college expenses, and a $485 rent note looming, I was frightened that I would never be able to make it on my own. I was, however, determined to move to Nashville!"

—R. J. Polca, Class of '94

26

TEMPING on the Web

The Internet has many work sites aimed at temps that can be navigated like an ordinary job search site; you can browse through temping jobs and agencies; post and update your résumé; and absorb enough job hunting tips, interviewing advice, and industry information to eventually launch yourself into a permanent position. Two sites worth your time are:

www.temping.com
Job listings are sparse due to the recent birth of this site, but the search function for temp agencies (over 20,000 sorted by zip code) is very good.

www.4temps.com
Besides offering job hunting tips, this site provides helpful advice specifically for temps and career shifters.

Temporary employment agencies are a great choice for people who want to learn about the world of work and get some experience at the same time. Working as a temp can provide you with flexibility and offers the opportunity to become more aware of your strengths and preferences. It also enables you to put bread on your table—maybe not croissants, but you will not be hungry! Temping allows you to get a firsthand look at what goes on in a variety of business settings. It offers an opportunity to learn more about your work preferences. A good many people are offered full-time employment after several months on the job as a temporary employee.

It's a good idea to talk with people you know who have had experience with temp agencies and ask them to suggest specific agencies that offer opportunities for wide exposure to work situations. It's important to investigate the firm's reputation. Is the agency a member of a professional organization, such as the National Association of Temporary Services? How long has the company been in your area? Which employers have utilized their services in the past? Does the agency provide paid lunch hours or group medical insurance? Be honest with the placement coordinator at the agency. Discuss your needs with reference to time to continue your job search, and don't forget to put your best foot forward and take your temporary assignments seriously. They could grow into full-time career opportunities.

27

DEALING WITH PARENTAL PRESSURE

Most parents will have a difficult time understanding your apprehensions about entering the job market and not starting on a "real career" immediately following graduation. They would love to be able to tell the neighbors, who frequently ask about your postgraduation plans, that you have a wonderful job with a great salary in an exciting industry. You're not the only one involved with peer pressures: Parents are vulnerable too!

Your challenge is to explain to your parents what you want to do and why. Let them know that most students really don't have a clear direction in mind when they graduate. Explain to them that you feel somewhat handicapped by your lack of focus, and that you'd like to explore options that will, in the long run, enable you to have a satisfying career.

Talk to them about how you reached your decision to try to identify your ideal job. You might even ask them about their life's work and talk about what field of work they would choose if they had to do it all over again. Most parents will understand your uncertainties and your need to explore. Many people of their generation made career choices for all the wrong reasons. They will certainly understand your need to investigate options, and will probably be supportive and particularly sympathetic to your situation.

The important thing is to communicate and to try to get them to understand where you're coming from. Indicate to them that you are very serious about finding the right field for yourself. Let them know that you have a plan of action and share that plan with them. Parents do have the ability to understand, and will often surprise you with their offers of assistance, both emotional and monetary.

"I began to feel pressured to find a job, but the pressure came from myself, not my parents. I felt that I owed it to them for giving me this great experience. I wanted to make them proud of me, but in fact, they already were. I remember my dad telling me not to worry, because 'Something will come up in time.' And it did. It wasn't as bad as I had anticipated. I wanted immediate results, but found I had to persevere and be patient."

—M. Tartaglione, Class of '94

FIRST WEEK ON THE JOB

During the latter part of our Reality 101 sessions, we always talked about the first day on the job—that is, the career job as opposed to an interim work situation. I will never forget one student's response to my standard question, "What really scares you about the first day of work in your chosen field?" Her lip quivered as she quietly replied, "Who will I have lunch with if I don't know a soul?" Her answer may seem absurd at first, but the thought of not knowing the ropes—and even something as trivial as finding a companion with whom to share lunch—was symptomatic of her many apprehensions about her new environment.

Making the transition from college to career is never easy. You're about to enter a new arena where the rules and regulations are totally unknown to you. Not only will you need to learn the specific duties you were hired to perform, but you will need to become aware of an entirely new cast of characters as well as the politics and philosophies of your workplace. The thought of the first week on the job is scary indeed. I can assure you that even the most confident new grads do more than a little nail-biting at this time, so relax, use your learning time constructively, and put your best foot forward.

Remember that you were hired because your employer believed you had the potential to become a contributing member of the organization. During your interviews, you demonstrated your ability to communicate effectively and to learn quickly. *Employers realize that new grads don't have the profes-*

> "The first week at work seemed like a month. The first month seemed like a year. But after a month, I couldn't believe how much I had learned."
>
> —S. Katzanek, Class of '85

sional skills needed to be immediately productive. All beginners make mistakes. Managers are aware that you will need time to assimilate all of the information to which you are being exposed. They expect the first few months on the job to be a time for listening, learning, and questioning, so don't pretend to have all the answers. You're really not expected to know it all—at first.

ASK AWAY, YOU'RE ALLOWED

The best way to learn what is expected of you, and what your supervisor wants, is to ask. What are the priorities, goals, and objectives of the organization? What will your duties be? Make sure your fully understand your job description. There is no such thing as a stupid question. Your boss will be more pleased if you ask about a special task and then do the job correctly than if you forge ahead blindly and later have to waste time redoing the whole thing. By the way, it's a good idea not to use your boss' first name at first. You might want to ask, "Shall I call you Ms. Jones?" Even if your boss asks you to use her first name, when speaking about her on the phone, or to a client visiting the office, always address her as Ms. Jones.

There is usually a formal meeting during your first week of employment when organizational policies and expectations are discussed. You will want to have a notebook with you at all times during the first few weeks of orientation (Yes, orientation once again!). Jot down all the relevant material presented to you and keep an ongoing list of questions you would like to ask. When you go home each night, review the material talked about that day and update any questions you might have, so that you can find the answers the following day.

This is the time to allow your positive attitude to be noticed. Display a willingness to learn and an enthusiasm for completing tasks, no matter how mundane they may be. If you've finished whatever task was assigned to you and have time on your hands, find something to do—you could read and reorganize existing files or acquaint yourself with correspondence relevant to your duties. You might use the time to review the company's personnel policies to make sure you are aware of the rules dealing with absence, lateness, or policies dealing with violations concerning drugs or ethics. You might ask to see a blank performance evaluation form, if possible, so that you will have some idea of what criteria is used in grading employees. (An evaluation is typically filled out after the first six months of your employment, and includes comments on your performance, initiative, attendance, etcetera.) Use your creativity to find a small project that you are capable of completing. In any event, keep busy, and keep away from the phone. Under no circumstances should you make personal phone calls!

A TIME TO LISTEN AND LEARN

Your competence and your attitude towards work assignments represent just one aspect of the total picture you're creating in your new workplace. The ability to fit in and to become part of the existing team represents the other portion of your professional persona, and it is equally important. The new professional who does well at specific assignments but who stands out because of pronounced differences and conflicts with the established employees will probably be job hunting again before the year is out.

You've undoubtedly belonged to numerous clubs in the past and had to work hard in order to really become a part of that team. Your current situation as a rookie employee is no different. Your antennae should receive information about the corporate culture to which you now belong. How do people dress? How do colleagues interact and communicate? How, and to whom, are new ideas presented? How are these ideas accepted by management? What are your co-workers' interests outside of the workplace? Do they read the books you enjoy and root for the same teams you do? Careful lis-

"Entering the real world is scary. Any time we have transition in our lives it's frightening. We're forced into life's rat race. My biggest fear is that I will have to compromise my dreams. I don't want life's hardships to coerce me into taking a job just to survive. What happens if I'm really not ready? I feel like my brain is a Whoopie cushion that has been sat on by a Sumo wrestler."

—J. Mitchell, Class of '97

tening and frequent interaction with your colleagues will help you understand the personal side of office dynamics and give you the confidence you'll need to become a full-fledged member of the team.

New professionals often try too hard to make a positive impression. They want to shine immediately and sometimes want to fix a system that doesn't need fixing. Find out which priorities are important to your boss, and follow the leader. It's usually best to keep your eyes and ears open and your mouth shut, until you've been with the organization for a while and have had an opportunity to really learn the ropes. Accept your role as new kid on the block, and learn all you can about your workplace. Criticizing existing methods or policies will surely alienate your co-workers. You will earn more points by listening, learning, and paying your dues as a rookie. Perhaps the best advice to new professionals is to become a good follower for the first year. Your leadership skills will be noticed and rewarded eventually.

FINDING A MENTOR

After you've been in the workplace for a month or two, try to define what you need in terms of your professional development. By this time, you've met a number of people in the organization and have interacted with several who understand your needs and can help you develop and grow professionally. It's important that you and your mentor are able to communicate easily and are on the same wavelength. Choose someone who not only has knowledge and influence within the organization, but who is also interested in helping you advance in your career.

After you have identified the person whom you think would be an ideal mentor for you, you will need to take steps to cultivate the relationship. Try to make a positive impression on your prospective mentor when the opportunity arises, at a company sponsored event, or even at coffee breaks. If you share similar interests, engage the person in conversation which relates to your mutual hobby or pursuit. Increase your visibility and provide opportunities for you to be observed. Demonstrate your competence and dress and act professionally.

The relationship between you and your mentor is a two-way street. Your mentor can benefit from your relationship as well. You can help her complete assignments while providing new ideas and energy to her projects. Remember to give your mentor feedback with reference to suggestions she's made. Remember too, to respect her very busy schedule and not take too much of her time.

View the first few months as time spent acquiring the knowledge, skills, and abilities you'll need to succeed in the workplace. If you adopt a positive attitude, build effective relationships, and understand your role as a new professional, your transition will be successful and exciting.

chapter 4

TO STAY, OR NOT TO STAY?

In chapter 3, we talked about the first week on the job, as well as some of the difficulties you're bound to encounter during the process of making the transition from college to the world of work. Let's assume that, as suggested, you've been doing your homework, trying to understand the culture of your workplace. You've observed your colleagues and learned a bit about how things are done in the company.

But after faithfully following all the "how to succeed" rules for the past six months, you're still wondering why things are not working out for you. You have to drag yourself out of bed in the morning. The thought of going to work is becoming increasingly depressing. You're wondering how you got yourself into this situation, and you may even be counting the years until retirement! Let's take a look at your dilemma, and try to reassess your situation.

Start by making a list, trying to identify those aspects of your life at work that are most unsatisfactory. Are you bored and dissatisfied with the work you do? Are you questioning the very nature of the tasks you perform each day? Do you feel that you haven't been given an opportunity to demonstrate your competence? Do you feel vastly underpaid for the work you do? Do you feel like an outsider? Have you been able to establish a satisfying social life outside of the workplace? What other factors contribute to your discontent? Perhaps your list will include some of the above issues—hopefully, it won't include all of them!

Before we examine your list, it's important for you to keep in mind that in our culture, young adults just out of college and in the process of launching new careers have concerns that are pretty much universal. First of all, people in their twenties are usually in the process of exploring relationships, both within and outside the workplace. Finding the right balance between their personal lives and work situations is a serious matter for most people in this age group as they become part of the work force. *Balance* is the key here. It's important for you to pursue new social situations and enjoy your life outside of your job. When all of your interests revolve around work, the result is bound to be boredom and burnout. You really do need to "get a life!"

YOUNG WORKERS POLL

Are they pessimists, or just realists? A recent AFL-CIO poll* revealed that young people are less than impressed with the country's employment outlook.

- Among workers between the ages of 18 to 34, fewer than half   45 percent—rated the economy as excellent or good, compared with 58 percent of those over age 35.

- More than half of young workers—58 percent—said employers are falling short when it comes to sharing profits with employees. A similar percentage, 55 percent, said companies aren't doing enough to provide family-friendly workplace policies.

- While more than 90 percent of young workers said they believe large corporations, top management and stockholders are doing well, 42 percent said the economic situation facing their own families is either "just fair," "not so good," or "poor."

- Only the youngest workers are willing to sacrifice job security for advancement opportunities: 42 percent of workers age 18–24 said job security is more important than advancement opportunities, compared with 63 percent of workers over age 35.

- 62 percent of workers age 18–24 said they believe that with education and hard work, a person can do well and get ahead. However, that drops to 52 percent by the time workers reach their early 30s.

- 45 percent of young workers often worry that their income won't keep up with the cost of living, and 42 percent often worry about incurring more debt than they can handle.

- Among the young workers polled, 50 percent of young women worry about having enough money for retirement, compared with only 37 percent of young men.

* The telephone survey of 752 young working adults, ages 18 to 34, was conducted in June 1999 by Peter D. Hart Research Associates. For comparison purposes, some questions were also asked of 401 workers ages 35 and older. The overall margin of error was plus or minus four percentage points.

Finding and establishing the appropriate level of commitment to a chosen career is very much a part of the postcollege adjustment, as well, and it's almost never an easy process. When I meet with young alumni who have graduated within the past five years, I am often struck by the sameness of their comments. *Everyone* is concerned about finding a career they will love. *Everyone* is concerned about their competence and ability to perform his or her job. *Everyone* becomes anxious about the unfamiliarity of a new workplace. *Everyone* soon becomes aware that school doesn't teach you everything. Few know how to deal with these concerns. Discovering how to find the necessary guidance, coaching, and support is an integral part of learning the ropes.

MAKING YOUR JOB WORK FOR YOU

Let's return to the list you've compiled. Your list, after you've reread it, should give you an indication of whether it's your entire profession or your particular employment situation that's causing your dissatisfaction. If your list includes lots of complaints about the small workspace you inhabit, the eccentricities of your boss, or the lack of challenging assignments, you might want to consider taking steps to remedy the specific situation. It is very possible for you to stay with the same company and create a plan to alleviate or change those aspects of your situation that are getting you down. Take some time and try to identify what you need to do in order to create opportunities that will demonstrate your competence. How can you be assigned more challenging work? Do you need advanced technical training? What steps do you need to take so that you can receive the assistance you need? It is vital that you identify, specifically, *what* you need, as well as *who* in the organization might be available to address those needs. In essence, what you're doing is a reality check, and a part of that process is realizing that there are virtually no jobs that are interesting, challenging, and exciting 100 percent of the time.

In chapter 3, we talked about the value of finding a mentor and establishing a relationship that will help you develop your talents at work. Having a mentor can make your life at work easier in so many ways. Your mentor can coach you in areas where you need guidance. She can help you gain exposure and visibility. She can help you understand the specific career paths in your organization, and point you in the right direction.

A mentoring relationship does not necessarily have to be formed with one individual. In her book *Mentoring at Work* (Scott, Foresman, 1985), Kathy Kram states, "Individuals in early career should consider several relationships that can provide some of the mentoring functions they need. Relationships with peers can also offer developmental functions, and individuals should develop a relationship constellation that consists of several relationships, each of which provides some career and/or psychosocial functions." Brenda Darby, an accountant who graduated in 1996, found two mentors in her first job: her supervisor and a senior accountant. They worked well together, as a team, and when one of the mentors left to go to another company, she urged Brenda to come along with her, which Brenda did. Mentors make great references!

You're probably wondering how you can identify and engage these veterans of the workplace who can help you gain confidence and become successful. *You* need to make it happen. Don't just stay in your office or cubicle and wait for someone to come knocking at your door to tell you what good work you've been doing. *You* need to seek out and initiate interaction with colleagues. Ask for feedback on projects with which you've been involved. It's also perfectly acceptable to ask for advice. The fact that you're willing to admit that you don't know it all demonstrates maturity on your part. After all, you are "the new kid on the block"— try to become comfortable with that role.

KNOWING WHEN TO CHANGE COMPANIES

If, however, you've been with your current employer for a year or more and have really tried to improve your situation, and your list indicates that you are happy with your chosen profession but really unhappy with the specific company you are working for, you might want to consider moving to another company in the same, or a related industry. Brenda Darby stayed with the same accounting firm for one and a half years after graduating. She was hired by the firm after completing her college internship, and she loved many aspects of her work. "I thoroughly enjoyed getting into my car each morning and going to work. I looked forward to working with really great people." When I questioned her about her reasons for deciding to move on, she responded, "If you stop learning and you're stuck doing the same thing most of the time, it's time to leave." Brenda believed that she could get more specific experience in the field of taxation elsewhere. Earning more money was not an issue for her; greater challenge and growth potential were the motivating factors.

Changing companies within the same industry is not as difficult as you might think. It's akin to transferring to another college after your freshman or sophomore year. In both instances, the record that you have established in your current institution can be either an asset or a liability, depending on how much you've accomplished and how well you've done your work. It is therefore important to continue to perform well, even though you're thinking of leaving the organization. So what are the steps you should take at this point?

Networking in a variety of settings usually puts you in touch with people who are aware of jobs that need to be filled. Participation in a professional organization in your specific field will enable you to come in contact with a good many employers, as well as other professionals. Spread the word that you are considering a job change, and be ready to discuss what responsibilities, ideally, you'd like your next position to include. *Be positive!* Never accuse, complain, or speak negatively about your present employment. Additionally, you should be aware that every professional organization publishes a newsletter that is distributed to its members at regular intervals. Job openings are frequently listed in these publications. You might even consider placing your own ad in the newsletter, to market your skills.

Don't limit your networking strictly to professional organizations and publications. You should consider taking a course, related to your career, at a local college. This will not only put you in touch with other professionals, but will also keep you up to date on numerous facets of your chosen field. If you are involved in any activities unrelated to your work, by all means share your job-changing plans with other volunteers or members of the group. You never know the extent of the relationships your friends and acquaintances have. You've probably heard of the "six degrees of separation" theory, whereby any person is connected to any other person through no more than six steps. I've tried to test this premise, and I must admit it does seem to work. I've been able (theoretically, at least) to contact religious leaders of the world, famous authors, even the President of the United States, by coming up with people I know, who know other people, and so on. Also, don't forget the importance of alumni from your college. Attending regional alumni events and keeping in touch with the Alumni Office will provide you with contacts who will be willing and able to help you. Just remember to write a thank-you note to anyone who has taken the time to talk with you.

Before you initiate your next job search, make sure you sit down and reassess your attributes. Don't allow your present position to limit your options. Think about your skills and interests, your values, your strengths. Have your values changed since you've entered the work force? What do you really care about? What do you enjoy most at work? Which parts of your daily routine do you dislike? Knowing what is truly important to you will enable you to consider a greater number of options for your next position. Also, you might want to examine the possibility of making a geographic change at this point in your career. Would you consider moving to another city, or another part of the country? Once you've decided it's the right time to move on, and you've completed an honest assessment of your strengths and weaknesses, you'll be adequately prepared to market yourself to a wide range of people.

A WHOLE NEW CAREER

We haven't yet talked about another scenario that might occur during the first year or so of your first job. Very possibly you have been quite happy with the social climate in your company. You enjoy being with your coworkers during work hours and you even socialize with them after work. It's a wonderful situation, except for the fact that you dislike most other aspects of your job! Perhaps you've had difficulty generating enthusiasm for most of the projects with which you've been involved. You're finding that the work you are doing requires too much attention to detail, which has never been one of your strengths. You're aware that creativity is one of your assets and truly miss having the opportunity to allow your creative juices to flow. You've begun to suspect that you are really not cut out for the "corporate life." You've discovered that your values are very different from those espoused by your company. Most important, you've been very observant, talked with colleagues in similar organizations, and are beginning to suspect that it's not just your company—it may be the *entire industry* that is just not right for you. I can't state actual percentages, but I have learned, from talking with a great many young alums, that it is not uncommon for people to realize, after they've been in the work force for a while, that they are just not suited for the career they chose right out of college.

It's time to go back to the drawing board and recreate your "ideal" day at work. Now that you have a more realistic picture of the day-to-day procedures in your company, when you try to visualize your day at work, which aspects of your daily routine would you still like to incorporate in your next job? Which functions did you really hate? Your negative experiences can be exceedingly helpful when you review your current career situation.

41

PERSONALITY TESTS on the Web

Do you feel there's a perfect career for you somewhere out there, but you have no idea what that career might be? A personality test or interest survey may help you by identifying your strengths and interests and tying them to potentially compatible careers.

For a thorough evaluation, you should contact a professional career counselor or visit a university career center. But you can get a rough sketch of your personality and interests by taking one of several online tests. These tests are often quick, fun, and fairly enlightening—you won't get an in-depth psychological profile, but you can come away with some new insights concerning "the real you."

Some sites worth trying:

www.queendom.com	www.personalitypage.com
www.keirsey.com	universityoflife.com
www.ansir.com	www.davideck.com

After you have determined that it's time to make that big change and pursue your dream job, start networking once again. At the same time, become a part of the temp world (where there is a critical shortage of qualified workers), conduct informal interviews with alums and other professionals, and continue to volunteer in organizations where you will be able to gain exposure to potential fields of employment.

The ball is now in your hands. It is absolutely possible for you to become an active player and winner in choosing the career that's right for you!

section **2**

starting your
NEW LIFE

chapter 5
MONEY AND YOUR LIFESTYLE

"The first year after college was a fairly easy transition for me. I had a job as a case manager, a roommate, and an apartment prior to graduation. This helped me feel like I had direction. It was very difficult financially, however. I was making about $18,000 working full-time and I had accumulated significant debt through college. This debt included student loans, credit cards, and leftover spring break balances. My parents were able to help me, but I wanted to be responsible for myself. I did not ask them for money unless I was really strapped. There were some weeks when I had zero in my bank account. That did make it easier to manage a budget, though. I just had to prioritize.

"I realized that my social life would be the first thing I needed to restructure. Next, I had to budget in major payments towards credit cards to pay off my debts. Surprisingly, that first year has taught me a lot about budgeting, and now my financial situation has improved. In addition, I now assist my clients who have lost their jobs with budgeting techniques. It's funny how certain skills can be very valuable later in life."
—M. P. Burke, Class of '92

How many times have you said to your friends, "I can't wait to be able to afford all those things we can't afford now"? The prospect of earning a

"I think the most difficult adjustment for me was to stick to a budget. I still use the budget form given to me in Reality 101 because it really is thorough. I just got a salary increase and used the form for the adjustment of my salary. Sticking to a budget was hard for me because I always wanted more. Now I have curtailed those cravings by allowing myself to save up for the item I want through savings."

—D. DeBenedetto, Class of '92

"real" salary, buying a new car, and getting a new wardrobe is really exciting, but don't forget that this new lifestyle is also going to include having to pay bills at the end of each month.

Once again, having a plan in place will help you deal with the new financial challenges you're about to face. This time the plan is called a *budget*. It's not easy to anticipate all the expenses your salary will have to cover, so putting the data on paper will help you see where your money goes.

You can use the monthly budget we used in Reality 101 as a guideline (see next page), and add or subtract items that pertain to your own expenses. You'll notice that the items listed in the top half of the budget are fixed expenses that *must* be paid monthly. The lower part of the paper deals with variable costs.

"The most difficult thing to adjust to was total independence. In college, you were on your own but you really weren't—there were always friends, roommates, and campus life. After graduation, it's all gone. You become truly self sufficient and responsible for your total well-being.

"Certain aspects of your life that you had never given much thought to before suddenly become very important. Things such as health insurance, financial security, and—if you are smart— retirement begin to play a major role."

—G. Maggiolino, Class of '94

CREDIT CARD DEBT

Banks make getting credit cards easy. Credit cards make spending easy. But sometimes easy is not so good. Credit card companies market extensively to recent graduates because there is a great deal of money to be made in that market: Interest rates vary from card to card and may range anywhere from 10 to 20 percent yearly. It's very easy for a new graduate to get caught in the credit card trap.

Before you accept or use your new credit card, make sure you *carefully read and understand the fine print* and can pay at least the monthly minimum balance. You should also be aware of some of the realities of owing money. For example, if you have a debt of $1,000 and make only

MONTHLY BUDGET

MONTHLY SALARY $_____

      Rent $_____

      Student Loan $_____

      Car Payment $_____

      Insurance:

          Car $_____

          Apartment $_____

          Health $_____

      Credit Cards $_____

      Telephone $_____

      Electricity $_____

      Heat $_____

      Transportation $_____

      Clothing $_____

      Savings $_____

      Entertainment $_____

      Food $_____

TOTAL OUTSTANDING $_____

SAVINGS LEFT OVER $_____

minimum payments, it could take you more than 15 years to pay it off and cost almost $2,000 in interest. The record numbers of people who have filed for personal bankruptcy should serve as a warning that easy spending can lead to big problems.

If at all possible, pay off your credit card debt as soon as possible. If you have a savings account or have received money as a graduation gift, you should consider paying off your credit card bills before you take that expensive trip you've been dreaming about. You can still plan an adventurous vacation that will not cost a great deal of money. "Pay now, buy later" is a good rule of thumb at a time when your income is limited.

Some grads choose to extend their student loans, which carry a lower interest rate, and use the money saved to lessen credit card debt. Paying off your debt as quickly as possible will make your new life a lot easier. There are some organizations that offer expert assistance with your financial concerns. The Consumers Credit Counseling Service (www.cccsintl.org) is a nonprofit organization that offers budgeting seminars as well as counseling for those who need help coping with finances. If you're in over your head and need help straightening out your financial situation, you can call the National Foundation for Consumer Credit at (800) 388-2227, or visit their Web site at www.nfcc.org. They will direct you to the counseling service nearest you. There is a fee for services based upon your ability to pay.

REPAYING STUDENT LOANS

Most students are troubled by the prospect of repaying their student loans. They're not sure of the who, what, when, and where of the system. I've asked Tracy Da Costa, a college financial aid counselor, to compile the following synopsis of the steps students should take after they graduate from college.

- Most important, all students who took out loans and signed promissory notes during their undergraduate study now have a legal obligation to repay that amount and any interest associated with that loan.

MONEY on the Web

Mom and Dad can't keep writing your checks forever! Learning to manage your own money is a big part of making it in the real world. Luckily, the Internet can help.

Online banking

Many banks are now offering personal online banking services to their account holders. If your bank is caught up with the technology of the Web, you can view your account balance, request transfers between accounts, and pay bills without leaving your computer. See your bank representative for more information.

ATM locator

Need cash in a hurry? Go to **www.mastercard.com/atm**, type in your address, and the ATM locator will map out the locations of the three ATMs closest to you.

Credit card info

Web guides such as **www.4creditcards.com** feature links to sites that allow you to obtain your confidential consumer credit report, apply online for major credit cards, or get free advice on getting out of credit card debt.

Money management

A wealth of helpful information is available online, including budget calculators, loan advice, sage investing/saving/spending strategies, and message boards and chat rooms to discuss your money questions. These four sites can help guide you through your fiscal faux pas:

moneycentral.msn.com	**www.bankrate.com**
www.moneyconcepts.com	**www.dca.org**

49

- All students are required to attend an exit counseling session at their college or university.

- Students should obtain loan information from all of their lenders, with reference to loan amounts and interest rates. Most schools will provide you with this information during your exit interview.

- Know the addresses and phone numbers of all your lending agencies.

- Know all of the loan repayment options that are available to you, such as loan consolidation, standard repayment, and graduated repayment. Choose the option that will best fall within the limits of your budget. (Note: These can be changed at a later date, once your income increases.)

- A *deferment* is the postponement of repayment of a student loan. As a borrower, you have a legal right to exercise this option if circumstances merit. There are several ways of qualifying for a deferment: One example would be enrolling in graduate school. Your loan counselor can advise you of other deferment options.

- *Forbearance* options are also available, where the lender agrees to extend your payment schedule to avoid a default situation. This option is based solely on the discretion of your lender. Contact your lender immediately if you are having problems with your repayment schedule. On certain occasions, lenders may be willing to temporarily change your repayment schedule.

- If you cannot make a payment for whatever reason, contact your lender. No one wins in a default situation, since your credit is marred and your lender loses out in getting his money back. So consider your lender a partner in trying to help you resolve these issues. Fortunately, the majority of students who borrow money also repay their loans without serious incident. This keeps interest rates low and allows the federal government to continue subsidizing these programs.

A word of caution is needed here about credit ratings. Anytime you are late with a payment, whether it be a credit card payment, car loan payment, telephone bill, or rent, it most likely will be reported to a credit bureau. This bureau will be contacted when you try to get a mortgage or want to borrow money to make any kind of sizeable purchase. *It's very important to remember that your buying and spending habits now may have major repercussions in the future.*

BUYING A CAR

If you thought you were finished with doing homework, think again. Making any major purchase requires lots of research before the transaction is completed. The process of buying a car is time consuming and takes lots of patience. It can be inconvenient and tiring, but hang in there—your persistence will pay off.

The first step is to decide whether you want a new or a used car. More and more people are buying used cars, since the initial cost of buying a used car is usually a good deal lower than the purchase of a new car. Insurance rates are also lower. In fact, auto industry sources estimate that nearly two thirds of all cars sold are used. Since car leasing has become more popular, many more used cars have entered the market as their leases expired. Purchasing a car that is just a few years old and has low mileage is a good way to keep your expenses down. Another benefit of buying a used car is the possibility of paying cash and avoiding finance charges.

A new development in the used-car business is the used-car superstore, where you can sit in the sales office and view the cars on a computer monitor instead of walking through a lot filled with cars. Most of the offerings are in excellent condition and come with a warranty. If you buy a vehicle from a reputable dealer, you will most likely get a warranty as well as background material on the car you're interested in. I checked with several dealerships that sell both new and used cars, and they assured me that they would put the potential buyer in touch with the previous owner if he would like additional information about a specific vehicle he's considering. You might also want to take the car to an independent mechanic to be checked out, especially if you're buying from a private party. This service usually costs between $50 and $100, but it is money well spent and can save you future headaches.

In any case, don't allow a salesperson to pressure you. If you start feeling hustled, ask to speak to another salesperson or perhaps even the manager. If you're not sure the car and the financial deal are right for you, you can put off making any decision. You need to feel confident about the person you're dealing with and about the car dealership, too.

Whether you're looking at a used or a new car, there are a variety of Web sites (see the sidebar on page 53) and books that can help you decide on the type of

"The most difficult adjustment for me was realizing that I had finally entered 'the real world.' This was what the past four years prepared me for. Now it was time to be responsible for myself and for my actions, so . . . sink or swim!"

—D. Conte, Class of '92

car that's best for you. You probably have consulted *Consumer Reports* (www.consumerreports.org) in the past for advice: The annual *Consumer Reports* Buying Guide Issue is a good source of information on all aspects of purchasing an automobile. You can learn, for instance, how much the car you're interested in cost the dealer, and the price of every option available for that car. That kind of information can be very helpful to you when you start negotiating with the salesperson, and will help you learn about the pros and cons of various cars. Information about costs of repairs, gas mileage, safety ratings, and resale values is also provided. Another widely used resource for previously owned cars is the National Automobile Dealers Association's *Official Used Car Guide* (www.nada.com/usedcarguide).

Before you buy a vehicle, you should spend time prioritizing the extras you want. Can you really afford a sunroof or that stereo system that has spectacular sound? It's true that such items will increase the resale value of your car, but they will also increase the purchase price.

Remember that the sticker price represents a suggested retail price of the car: A dealership is not legally obligated to sell the car at this price. Most dealers will sell below their sticker price. Other dealers and manufacturers like Saturn will not accept lower offers.

Prepare a worksheet and write down the base price of the car you're interested in as well as the price of each option you'd like to have. If you've done your homework, you will know the exact wholesale cost of the car you'd like to drive away in. The difference between the wholesale and the sticker price gives you some room to negotiate.

There are a number of books and videos available at your local library that can help you acquire good negotiation skills. If you are not adept at negotiation but one of your friends is, it might be a good idea to invite your friend to join you on your car-buying safari. I always ask my daughter to accompany me when I'm ready to purchase a car. Not only does she do a superb job negotiating, but she truly enjoys the process.

Every dealer has his own type of financing programs. Many dealers have

CARS on the Web

The Internet has become a popular tool for researching new and used cars. Here is just a sample of the resources available to you online:

Comprehensive info

Directories such as **carpoint.msn.com**, **www.autoweb.com**, and **www.4autos.com** offer you a broad range of automobile information.

Pricing guides

Kelley Blue Book—The industry standard of car-buying guides is now online at **www.kbb.com**.

Consumer Reports—Annual ratings of various cars can be found at **www.consumerreports.org/Categories/CarsTrucks/index.html**.

National Automobile Dealers Association's *Official Used Car Guide*—For the widely respected guide to used cars, go to **www.nada.com/usedcarguide**.

Leasing

Explanations on how leasing works, advice for consumers, and tools to help you get the best possible deal can be found on sites such as **www.leaseguide.com**.

Dealerships

Dozens of dealers have Web sites that allow you to search by car model and/or geographic region; you can also e-mail them a description of exactly what you're looking for. (But make sure the dealer is reputable before making any commitments!)

Financing

Lenders' sites include standards such as Ford Credit (**www.fordcredit.com**) and Chrysler Financial Corporation (**www.chryslerfinancial.com**). Many sites offer online loan applications. Again, know who you're dealing with to avoid being "taken for a ride"!

Auto insurance

Use a Web guide such as **www.4autoinsurance.com** to shop around for competitive insurance rates.

rebates for new graduates and first-time buyers. Sometimes these programs are not advertised, so you'll have to inquire about them. You should definitely look into financing your car through your bank, but carefully investigate promises of low monthly payments to the dealership. Again, do your homework and shop around until you find a rate that fits into your budget. Remember that even though the sales contract binds you to the new car's purchase price and the trade-in value of your old car (if you trade one in), the contract has no bearing on the source of payment. So even if you sign up for the dealer's finance package, you can still apply to a bank or credit union for a loan to pay off the dealer.

If you can manage to sell your old car privately, you'll probably get a better price. But if you don't, avoid talking with the dealer about your old car until you've settled on the purchase price of a new one. Generally, you'll get a better deal if you talk about the value of the trade-in last. There are a number of guides available at libraries and newsstands and on the Internet that will give you an idea of what your trade-in is worth.

Before you buy a new car, it is important to know the cost of insurance for the car. Here, too, you should investigate several insurance companies and learn what services they provide, how much deductible you will have to pay, etcetera. A friend or relative who is knowledgeable in this area would be a great resource person to consult. Car insurance rates vary according to your age, driving record, marital status, and geographic area, but the average insurance for a 22-year-old male with a clean driving record is probably between $1,300 and $1,800 a year. It is somewhat less for women.

When it's time to pick up your car, you will have to sign all loan agreements, have a certified check for your down payment, and have a check made out to the Registry of Motor Vehicles for the registration of your car. You will need some sort of verification from your insurance company to indicate that the car is insured. If you are receiving a recent graduate rebate, you will need a copy of your diploma as well.

Leasing a car is probably not the best option for you if you're just starting out. The down payment and the monthly payments will be lower and your car will be a fairly new one, but you won't own the car and there is a

"When I worked at a multinational consulting firm, I had to adhere to their strict corporate attire code. I started my business wardrobe by buying a black suit and a blue suit. I built it from there by adding different blouses, skirts, and scarves."

—D. DeBenedetto, Class of '92

54

penalty for early termination of the contract. Also, insurance rates are usually high and there is often a limited-mileage clause in the contract. The dealers I consulted do not recommend leasing for new graduates unless you travel for your work and are compensated for the mileage.

One final word about cars. If you plan to live in a large city that has a fairly good transportation system, you might consider not having a car for now. It is probably a lot cheaper for you to rent a car when you leave the city to visit friends or go on vacation than to deal with the costly insurance, parking fees, and frequent break-ins that have become a part of city life. You should consider all options before committing to costly payments each month, and remember, if you've made the wrong choice, you can always go to Plan B or even Plan C if necessary.

BUILDING A PROFESSIONAL WARDROBE: SOMETIMES A BOOK *IS* JUDGED BY ITS COVER

Part of the visualization exercise in the previous chapter involved picturing yourself getting dressed for your ideal job. Now that you're almost ready to try out that job, what kind of clothes will you need and, just as important, what impact will buying these clothes have on your budget?

You've probably heard the term *corporate culture* and are aware that it refers to the specific style of the people who work at any given organization. Dress codes will vary greatly, depending on the industry and management team at the helm of a business. Careers in the creative world, publishing, advertising, art, or dance, will generally allow you to exhibit creativity in your dress. This creativity is viewed as an extension of your ability to generate ideas and demonstrate your artistic bent. Showcasing your creativity in your attire is certainly acceptable. On the other hand, insurance companies, banks, and law offices expect a more conservative manner of dress from their employees. Sometimes businesses actually have guidelines that specifically indicate the dos and don'ts of office attire.

If you're not sure you're dressing right on the job, look around you and notice the attire of the managers and others who are the decision makers. It's always safe to ask if there is an unwritten dress code for employees.

Meanwhile, wear your more conservative clothes until you get a sense of what's appropriate. As always, if you wear something you feel good in, you won't spend needless energy worrying about your appearance.

We've heard the phrase *dress for success* many times, but how do you manage to buy a wardrobe for your new work situation while you're living on a very tight budget? Once again, you'll need to devise a plan.

You really don't need to buy a great many clothes. Start with the basics and add new components and accessories from there. For men, interesting ties can change the look of a suit that is worn fairly often. Women can vary the jewelry, scarves, or blouses they wear with that basic suit. The mix-and-match rule will help you recycle the same outfits until you can afford to augment your wardrobe.

There are a good many discount type stores where you can shop without paying a premium price for your clothes and accessories. Try to buy as good a quality item as you can afford. Think of buying clothes that are "classic" and not in a style that will be out of fashion next year. An expensive suit that you can wear for five or six years is a better investment than a poorly made bargain that looks shabby after you've worn it for a year or two.

Resale shops offer interesting selections of apparel for a fraction of the price you would pay for new merchandise. Here, again, ask around so you know which stores carry the better quality clothes. An increasing number of new graduates are finding that resale shopping is a great way to stay within their budgets.

Helen Gurley Brown, former editor of *Cosmopolitan*, said in a magazine article, "Nearly every glamorous, wealthy, successful big-time career woman you envy now started out as some kind of schlep." If you put some time and effort into planning a wardrobe, *you* won't have to start as a schlep!

chapter 6
LEASES, LANDLORDS, AND LIABILITIES

Finally, you've graduated and are ready for a place of your own and some real independence. A place of your own can become a reality, but you need to look very carefully at the costs involved in this move.

Budget experts agree that your monthly rental should normally amount to no more than your weekly (gross, before taxes) salary. In other words, if your salary is $2,000 a month, your budget will allow you to spend about $500 for rent. If you follow this formula, does your budget allow you to rent and maintain an apartment on your own, or is it unrealistic to do so? Most of the new graduates I know could not manage, financially, to live without one or two roommates. You may have dreamed of a place of your own, but that dream may have to be deferred for a while. Besides, sharing an apartment with the right person or persons can be a very positive experience.

Again, you will need to think about your priorities and determine which issues dealing with the quality of your life are most important to you at this time. If you have $500 a month to spend on rent and you *must* live alone, would you consider leasing a very small, studio-type apartment?

Would you consider living in a house with an elderly person, where you would have your own room or rooms, possibly rentfree, in exchange for providing prearranged services? There are many possibilities out there. Creatively exploring your options can be fun once you're sure of the direction you'd like to pursue.

It's a good idea to prepare a checklist of those things that are important to you in your search for housing. Some of the items to consider are safety, parking, laundry facilities, the availability of public transportation, and the possibility of renting a furnished apartment. Later on, when you start looking at a number of places, you'll want to consult this list.

WHEN AND WHERE TO LOOK

Start looking for an apartment as soon as you know where you will be living after graduation. Keep your eyes and ears open and communicate your needs to friends and relatives. The best way to locate a suitable apartment is through word of mouth: Not only can you learn about the good and bad points of the rental firsthand, but you will be able to avoid a realtor's fee, which could be sizeable. So start spreading the news!

Many newspapers have specific days of the week when rental listings are published. Saturday and Sunday are usually the best days to look in daily papers. You may want to check publication dates for suburban newspapers, which are usually published weekly or biweekly.

Check out bulletin boards in your college if you're going to remain in the area. If you're moving to another location, you might want to contact colleges in that vicinity. Hospitals, too, often have listings of available apartments as well as notices posted by staff who are seeking roommates. We'll talk about roommate selection later on.

The local Yellow Pages of the telephone directory can provide you with a list of real estate agencies that can help you locate housing. Usually, there is a "finder's fee" charge for the realtor's service. In some geographic areas, however, it is customary for the landlord to pay the fee. Make sure you understand what the situation is before you go to look at any apartments. Fees can range from $50 to a full month's rent, and they *can* be negotiated. It's always a good idea to let the realtor know what your price range is before you start looking at apartments.

Once you find a suitable apartment, be prepared to pay the first and last month's rent before you move in. Sometimes you will also have to pay a security deposit that will be set aside to cover any damages to the apartment during your stay. You may want to check with the local housing

APARTMENT HUNTING on the Web

Apartment hunting on the Internet is not for the financially challenged; the majority of Internet listings focus on luxury apartment complexes and communities. Your best bet for locating affordable housing in your area is the local newspaper or rental agencies (both of which may be found online, with a little searching). But for those of you with cash to spare, check out these reputable sites:

www.Rent.net   www.apartments.com

www.aptguides.com   www.springstreet.com

www.aptsforrent.com

Helpful features include: photos of buildings; amenities information; floor plans (some with 360-degreee virtual tours); roommate listings; contacts for relocation services such as rental trucks, supplies, and storage units; and moving tips and advice.

authority so you can learn the rules governing security deposits, such as the maximum dollar amount allowed, returning the deposit after you've moved out of the apartment, and the possibility of accrual of interest on the deposit while it is in the hands of the landlord.

It's important that you carefully inspect the apartment and make note of any existing damage. You probably have experience filling out housing inventory forms for your college's Office of Student or Residential Life. Create a similar list, have the landlord sign it, and make sure you have a copy. One realtor who specializes in rentals suggests that you videotape any damage you notice in the apartment before you move in. This will give you a visual record of damages you shouldn't have to pay for when you are ready to move on.

DEPOSITS

When you start looking at apartments, make sure you have a checkbook with you. If you find a place you really like, you will have to put a deposit on it as soon as possible. Deposits can range from $50 to a full month's rent, and should always be applied to your first month's payment. It's a good idea to find out if the money is refundable in case you change your mind and, if so, how long it will remain refundable.

Before you write that check, take out that list of priorities you made before you started searching actively. Does this apartment or house offer those things which are important to you? This is also the time to get any additional information you'd like about the rental. Some questions you might ask include:

- What is the average monthly cost of utilities?

- How is the place heated, by gas, oil, or electricity? What appliances are permitted?

- Are utilities included in the monthly rent?

- Does the landlord permit pets?

- Who lives in the same house? On the same floor?

- What does the landlord expect of you as a tenant?

- Is the neighborhood fairly safe?

If you're not sure of the neighborhood, you might want to call or visit the local police station where you can get additional information about the general safety of the area. Don't be afraid to ask about the nature of crimes committed in the area. Are most offences merely parking tickets and traffic violations, or have there been a rash of robberies in the neighborhood recently? I know a number of people who have consulted the police and received helpful advice concerning areas to avoid. Alumni, too, can be helpful in steering you in the right direction as far as neighborhood and safety are concerned. Don't hesitate to contact your college's alumni office and get a listing of people who live in the area you're considering.

LANDLORDS

It's helpful for you to know that landlords fall into several categories. An *owner-occupant* is someone who owns and lives on the property you are renting. This kind of landlord is usually very interested in keeping the property in good condition, and will probably expect you to do the same. On the positive side, the owner-occupant is most often around when you need to have repairs made in your apartment. Sometimes, however, you may feel that your privacy is being invaded. It's a good idea to communicate with the landlord and work out rights and privileges from the start. Can he enter your apartment at any time, or must you be home? How does she feel about your inviting several friends to stay with you for a weekend? These certainly are not major issues, but it is always helpful to know what the rules are.

If you choose to move into a large apartment complex, you will most likely deal with a professional landlord or superintendent who lives in the complex and makes repairs when you need them. Here, too, it's a good idea to find out what kind of access this person has before you sign the lease. You might also want to ask about the neighbors: Are there other young people in the complex? Are there any facilities on site for working out? If not, how far away if the nearest gym?

An *absentee landlord* is one who does not live in the building he rents. If this is the case, it's important to know whom to call when things break and need repair. You may want to contact the previous tenant and inquire about the maintenance of the property and the landlord's response to requests made by the tenant. If there are other apartments in the complex, you could also ask one of the neighbors about the landlord's track record when it comes to the caliber of services performed. If you get some negative feedback, you may want to continue your search elsewhere.

LEASES

A *lease* is similar to the housing contract you signed if you lived on campus: This time, though, it is a contract between tenant and landlord instead of an agreement between student and college. A lease is considered a legal document, so pay close attention to its content. It should clearly state your

SAMPLE LEASE

LESSEE/LESSOR   This indenture of lease made this _____ day of _____1998 by and between _____, hereinafter referred to as Tenant, and _____, hereinafter referred to as Landlord.

WITNESSETH

(1) ADDRESS OF PROPERTY/TERM RENT: That in consideration of the premises, rents, and covenants herein esxpressed, Landlord hereby leases Tenant and Tenant rents from Landlord, upon the terms and conditions set forth,

ADDRESS_____

    TERM: _____ TO _____

    TOTAL SUM: $_____

FIRST INSTALLMENT OF $_____ DUE BEFORE OCCUPANCY AND ACKNOWLEDGE AS RECEIVED WITH APPLICATION.
    PRO-RATA RENT FROM _____ TO _____ IS $_____ SUBSEQUENT INSTALLMENTS OF $_____ ARE DUE ON THE _____ DAY OF EACH CALENDAR MONTH THEREAFTER WITHOUT NOTICE, DEMAND, OR DEDUCTION.

(2) PAYMENTS: Rent shall be payable to _____ if they are managing the property. If the property is not professionally managed, rent is payable to the Landlord at his address as follows:

_____

Landlord's Phone Number: _____

(3) LATE FEE/COST OF RETURNED CHECKS: If any installment of rent is not received by Agent or Landlord within _____ days from the due date, Tenant covenants and agrees to pay as additional rent the sum of $_____. Tenant further agrees to pay a handling charge of $20.00 for each check returned by the bank for insufficient funds or any other reason. landlord or Agent may require any and all payments to be made in cash, money order, or certified funds.

(4) OCCUPANTS USE: Tenant will use said property as a single family residence for _____ person(s) and for no other purposes or additional number of persons whatever, except children born hereafter and temporary guests, without prior written consent of Landlord or Agent. Temporary guests are those persons who occupy proprty for not more than four (4) weeks during any twelve-month period. This lease shall not be assigned nor any portion of the premises sublet, without prior written consent of Landlord or Agent.

(5) GOOD REPAIR: Except as otherwise provided herein, Landlord will maintain the said property in good repair and tenantable condition, and will be responsible for all major repairs not due to the fault or negligence of the Tenant during the continuance of this lease. Repairs of replacement of equipment provided due to normal wear and tear shall be at the expense of the Landlord. Tenant shall keep the premises, including all plumbing fixtures, facilities, and appliances as clean and safe as condition permits and shall unstop and keep clear all waste pipes, drains, and water closets thereon. The Tenant expressly covenants and agrees that at the termination of the lease, all appliances and equipment will be in good working order and shall be operative, and that the premises will be in good clean condition, ordinary wear and tear expected. All utility services shall be taken out of Tenant's name before any part of the security deposit can be returned. The Tenant is reponsible for loss or damage from freezing of water pipes or plumbing fixtures or from the stopping of water closets and drains which shall be repaired at the expense of the Tenant, unless the cause is beyond the Tenant's control.

Tenant shall use in a reasonable manner all electrical, plumbing, sanitary, heating, ventilating, air-conditioning, stove, refrigerator, and other fixtures, facilities, and appliances in the premises, and Tenant shall be responsible to repair them at his expense for any damage caused by his failure to comply with this requirement.

(6) PETS: Tenant shall not keep or allow pets on premises without consent of Landlord or Agent. The following pet(s) may be kept on the premise:_____
The Tenant agrees to arrange for and pay the cost of having the house treated by a professional exterminator, and the existing carpeting professionally cleaned at the termination of occupancy, should the above consent be given for fur-bearing pets. Paid receipts must be provided to Landlord or Agent. Tenant further agrees to assume all liability and to be responsible for any damage cuased by said pet(s), such as odor and damage to carpets, screens, glass, and home.

No modification or addition to this agreement shall be binding unless signed by the parties hereto.

63

rights and responsibilities. In order to be a binding contract between you and a landlord, a lease should contain the following items:

- The address of the premises, with a brief description of the number of rooms

- The names of the lessor and lessee

- The length of time of the lease, or *term of occupancy*

- The amount of the monthly rent, when it is due, and to whom it is paid

- Signatures of landlord and tenant

These five provisions make up a standard lease. The remainder of the lease usually consists of tenant responsibilities, and is known as the *fine print*. Here again, as with your credit card contract, it's important to make sure you read the fine print carefully. Also, be sure to keep a copy of the lease in a safe place so that you can refer to it if questions arise later on.

An example of what a lease looks like appeared on the previous two pages. This is a very short, abbreviated version of a lease—to give you an idea of how much it *doesn't* say, this lease omits any mention of the security deposit, commission fees for a real estate agent, renewal fees, provisions for default, attorney's fees in cases of future dispute, general maintenance, utility charges, redecoration procedures, liability for damage, trash removal, the storage of explosives and inflammable substances, and other matters both essential and trivial.

FINDING AND KEEPING A ROOMMATE

"Two months after graduation, I landed a great job in Boston working for an up-and-coming advertising agency. I had been living at home with my parents, and it was starting to take its toll. After all, I had spent the last four years on my own, and being back at home created a sense of

dependency all over again. Well, I was determined to be independent again! Since I didn't know anyone living in the Boston area, my boyfriend (who was already living in Boston with three other guys) suggested I move in with his friend's mother, whom I had met only once. She was looking for someone to share her large house with. So, having no other options, I took her up on her offer.

"I had my own bedroom and bathroom in the lower level of the house, and had full use of the kitchen and living areas. It was nice . . . for a while. But after a couple of weeks, I found that I'd assumed the role of best friend to this middle-aged woman. She expected me to go grocery shopping with her, eat all my meals with her, and watch television with her. I soon had no life of my own. Oh yes, there was also a pet snake in the laundry room. (Did I mention that I have a severe phobia of snakes)? Needless to say, I moved out after two months.

"Next, I decided to try my luck with the classified ads. After all, there are always ads for people wanting roommates in a big city. I found an ad placed by a woman who was looking for another woman to share a two-bedroom, two-bath apartment. It was five minutes from the 'T' train and had a fitness facility, swimming pool, and shuttle service. Best of all, it was already furnished. It was a great apartment! I didn't know this woman, but had to act quickly to escape from my other situation and she seemed nice. So I hastily signed the rental agreement.

"Things were fine for the first year. I went about my usual business, spent time with my boyfriend, and occasionally went out with my new roommate. After a while, I noticed that she had a tendency to borrow my clothing—lingerie, in particular. She also had many visitors coming at different times of the day and night. These visitors—all men—were supposedly 'friends' of my roommate, and would keep me up all hours of the night (for obvious rea-

"Adjusting after college was not too rough for me. I lived here in Bristol, the town where my college was located, for the summer after graduation. I found that it wasn't the same: The people I knew weren't around, the local hangouts looked different, and I realized that it was time to move on."

—K. Deckert, Class of '96

sons). Once, I came home from work one day to find my roommate and one of her 'friends' in my bed!

"After two job changes, I realized that advertising was not the field for me and decided to return to school for a master's degree. The school I chose was back in my hometown, so I moved back in with my parents. They have been my best roommates so far!"
—K. Meghreblian, Class of '92

Leaving college after four or five years is never an easy step to take. The thought of moving to a new area, finding suitable housing, and choosing the right person to share that housing with intimidates most new graduates. So if you're feeling overwhelmed by the whole process, you're certainly not alone.

It's a good idea to start talking about your postcollege plans and options in the spring semester of your last year on campus. I can assure you that most of your classmates are faced with the same dilemma as you. They probably don't have jobs waiting for them, they don't want to return to their parent's home, and they're not sure whether to hang around the college town or venture out into a new area. If you get the word out among your friends, you'll probably find other graduates interested in moving to the same city you'd like to live in. Many new grads find compatible roommates by networking and discussing their plans for the following year with others who are in a similar situation.

If you've lived in a dorm, you already know exactly the kind of person you'd like to avoid having as a housemate. So now you should consider the traits you'd like your ideal roommate to have. Try to prioritize them: How important is neatness? Is responsibility high on your list? Would it matter if the person had friends sleep over often? How high is your tolerance for loud music? Sometimes sharing your criteria for a roommate with a group of people helps you get in touch with your own strong feelings and degrees of tolerance.

If you are moving to a new area, need a roommate, and don't know of anyone who wants to share an apartment, where do you turn? Most large cities have agencies that help people find suitable roommates. There is always a fee for this service, but the agency usually screens applicants and will try to find someone who is compatible. It's important that you keep your list of priorities in mind when interviewing your potential housemate. Don't be afraid to ask any questions you may have about the person's lifestyle, their phone habits, or how often their friends will visit. What is your initial impression of this potential roommate? Do you think he or she will fit in with your lifestyle?

It's really important that you talk about the rules of the household that are important to you. People's responses to your questions should give you some indication of whether their personalities and values are compatible with yours. Sometimes your gut reaction to a situation will help you make the right decision.

Local newspapers often run ads placed by people who want to share their living quarters. Most of these ads are perfectly legitimate and can help you find suitable housing. It's always a good idea, however, to phone the person who has placed the ad before you inspect the premises. Again, if your gut reaction is negative after talking with the person, don't pursue that situation. You can also take the initiative by placing an ad in the local

HOW TO . . . ? on the Web

So you know how to finish a 30-page term paper in one night, but don't know which fork goes with dessert? Use the Web to find tips for getting by in the real world.

- If you've ever felt clueless about ANYTHING involving automobiles, cooking, health, homemaking, etcetera, here's an answer to your prayers. Just visit one of these sites for in-depth tutorials on topics ranging from the esoteric ("how to seed a pomegranate") to the practical ("how to replace a hubcap") to the necessary ("how to tie a necktie"):
  www.how2hq.com   **www.ehow.com**   **www.learn2.com**

- Agonizing over the color of your bathroom? Anxious about hosting a dinner party without a dining room? Be sure to check out **www.ApartmentLife.com** for your most dire apartment-related emergencies. This site for the low-budget recent grad is full of fun tips on entertaining, decorating, and making the most of your new living space.

newspaper. This will allow you to interview a number of people who respond to your ad and choose the one you find most suitable. Bulletin boards in colleges, local hospitals (where medical staff often look for roommates), and of course, contacting alumni who live in the area are other resources you should consider in your search for a roommate.

If you are successful in finding a roommate, it is *essential* that both of you sign the lease provided by the landlord. If, for any reason, your roommate moves out before signing the lease, *you* will be responsible for paying all of the bills. It's important, too, to discuss the financial arrangements concerning phone usage, groceries, and any other household expenses incurred. Once again, having a checklist and establishing rules before you settle in will make life a lot easier later on.

I know a number of recent grads who have had great roommates. I also know a few who have horror stories about their experiences. If you find yourself in the latter category after a few months on your own, start thinking of a Plan B, and implement it as soon as possible. Consider the negative episode a valuable learning experience!

chapter 7

FINDING FRIENDS, FUN, AND PHYSICIANS

Leaving college and friends who are like family is never easy. In fact, most seniors place this issue near the top of their list of concerns. You've had a very good life for the past four or five years, finding good friends and establishing great relationships. Not knowing the future is pretty frightening by itself, but facing the unknown without your support system of friends can be truly terrifying.

For a good many people, transitions and change are always accompanied by anxiety. Remembering how you dealt with previous changes in your life can help you adjust more quickly to your current situation. Try to identify and verbalize exactly what you will be leaving when you graduate. Which aspects of your current life do you think you will miss the most? What do you expect in your new situation? Also try to recall your personal history of transition and loss. Was leaving high school really hard for you? If your parents are divorced, how did you deal with that? Have you witnessed the death of a parent, grandparent, or good friend? How did you react to these losses? Did it take you a very long time to get over the sorrow?

"When I was a senior, the most frightening aspect of leaving college was losing my friends. I had developed very close relationships within my circle: We were friends from the first day we met through graduation. I lived with the same roommate all four years. The thought of starting over and making new friends was scary. We all felt that we would be alone in the 'real world.' It was like the first day of college all over again. We did not know what was ahead of us—all we knew was that our lives were changing. This time, however, we needed to start our own individual journeys."

—M. P. Burke, Class of '92

69

Becoming aware of your special manner of handling past changes in your life will help you deal with your current transitions. You have survived change in the past, and you will do so again. You need to be realistic and acknowledge the fact that meeting new people will probably take some time and effort. You also need to realize that your college friends are forever.

The year following graduation is filled with many adjustments, some easier to make than others. Once you've decided on a career direction (for now), moved into your apartment, and started working, what are you going to do for fun, and with whom? How are you going to meet people your own age, who have the same interests as you?

"It's been three years since I graduated, and I still keep in touch with my closest college friends. I have already attended two weddings and am going to another next July. We have promised to stay in touch and visit one another as often as possible. We established what we like to call 'Girls Weekend.' We get together at someone's house every two or three months to laugh, reminisce, and catch up on one another's lives. We've been successful in maintaining our close friendships, and after countless miles traveled and hundreds of dollars in long-distance calls, we've proven that friendships can and will continue if you want them to."

—M. Tartaglione, Class of '94

Some recent grads report that there have been people at work with whom they could "connect" and socialize. In some instances, however, all the employees are a good deal older, which usually limits socializing to the workplace. Some of these older co-workers will be very supportive and may introduce you to people your age within their network of friends and family. I know a number of people who have become good friends with and been "adopted" by older co-workers. This closeness helped make the transition from college to the workplace fairly easy. Also, remember that your college friends are still there for you. They're probably facing a similar situation and need your support as much as you need theirs. You may not be able to sit in the dorm, chatting for hours at a time, but the phone and the computer make frequent communication and support fairly easy.

REACHING OUT TO FIND NEW FRIENDS

Once again, volunteering can help you achieve your goal. People of similar interests are usually attracted to the same type of volunteer opportunities, so choosing a volunteer site will give you the opportunity to meet interesting people. Were you interested in being a Big Sister or Big Brother while you were in college, but perhaps couldn't find the time to become involved? If you love animals, and are not allowed to have a pet in your apartment, would you consider helping out at the local Animal Rescue League? Have you ever thought about working in a soup kitchen? Would you consider teaching Sunday School in your place of worship? Does giving guided tours of historic areas in a city interest you? Have you always wanted to spend more time with elderly people? There are literally hundreds of volunteer situations available for you to explore, and some of them will even pay you. Use your creativity as you select an organization that will help you become involved in your new community. There is no need to sit at home on weekends and wallow in self-pity.

Most cities have at least one agency that serves as a clearinghouse for volunteer activities. As mentioned in chapter 1, The Points of Light Foundation in Washington, D.C. (800-750-7653) can put you in touch with a local volunteer agency. Reaching out and doing something that really interests you will enable you to meet friends who have the same values and interests. It's a great way to meet new people. If sports is your thing, coaching a local softball, soccer, basketball, or hockey team will allow you to meet new people and also to stay in shape. The recreation board of your city or town can supply you with a complete listing of activities revolving around sports. Also, the local YMCA/YWCA can provide you with the opportunity to join various sports leagues. Participating in exercise classes or working out in a fitness center are also good ways to meet people of similar interests. Joining a gym is a good idea, but it can be costly. You may want to do some comparative shopping and investigate the special deals available at any given time: Most gyms periodically offer trial memberships for newcomers.

Attending religious services at a local place of worship is a very good way to meet people. There are always opportunities for participation in young peoples' groups in most synagogues and churches. Most communities have drama and reading clubs that might be of interest to you. If there is no reading group already in existence, you could take the initiative and start a book club. You could enlist two or three people who would be interested in joining. Most book clubs read one book a month and meet at a member's house, or perhaps in a cafe, to discuss the current selection. I have been a participant in a book club for about ten years, and have enjoyed many interesting, impassioned discussions with great people whom I probably wouldn't have had the opportunity to meet elsewhere.

You might consider taking an evening course at a local college or high school. Adult education offers many opportunities to explore and develop hidden talents and pursue areas of interest. If you'd rather not get bogged down in the academic arena, you might consider taking a course in cooking, photography, or watercolor techniques. There are endless opportunities to explore interests you never had time for while you attended school.

If you're like most people just out of school, your apartment will probably be furnished with hand-me-downs, lawn furniture, and other assorted acquisitions. If you're a fix-it person, or if decorating or finding interesting antiques interests you, why not spend some time cultivating and exploring those hobbies? Not only will you learn a great deal about a particular subject, but you will also acquire interesting furnishings that are probably not too expensive.

This is a great time to investigate something new or something you've always wanted to do but, for whatever reasons, have never gotten around to. Participation in a new activity will give you an opportunity to meet interesting people and gain new skills that will enhance your sense of personal well-being. In your student days, it was important to exercise and deal with the stress of studying for exams. At this time in your life, it is equally important for you to balance the stress you accumulate at your job with interesting activities that are fun to do and are not very expensive. Your mind and body need to be cared for, and it's up to you to to make sure there is balance in your life.

If you tended to be a person who partied frequently, drank a good deal of alcohol, stayed up late, and took naps to catch up on your rest, you will need to re-examine your habits and initiate change. To be successful in whatever field of work you choose, it's important that you drink less, sleep more, and have a reasonable diet. This may sound like a radical idea, but 100 percent of the recently graduated people I talk with indicate that integrating exercise and good nutrition into their new lifestyle is of prime importance, and is related to being successful at their jobs.

FINDING HEALTH INSURANCE AND RECEIVING GOOD HEALTH CARE

At college, you turned to the Health Services office when you weren't feeling well. How do you handle illness when you are living hundreds of miles from home, don't have a family doctor, and really need to talk with or be examined by a health professional?

You're undoubtedly well aware of the massive changes the health care delivery systems in this country have undergone. Hospitals are merging, hospitalization for all but critically ill patients is practically nonexistent, and insurance companies are playing an increasingly major role in today's health care. Visiting the doctor who lives in your neighborhood may no longer be an option because of the many changes in the rules governing health insurance. There are, however, basic facts you need to be aware of in order to be eligible to receive good medical care if and when you need it.

"After graduation, your priorities change drastically. You tend to become more conscious of things that you normally took for granted, such as spending patterns, sleep, and more importantly, free time. I remember that if I was tired in college, I'd take a nap. If I'm at work, a nap isn't really an option. You become very aware of your basic needs. When I first began working, I used to get burnt out very quickly and soon became aware that I could not stay up all night and go out like I used to do when I was in college."

—G. Maggialino, Class of '94

You were probably covered by your parents' health insurance plan while in school. In most cases, you will not be eligible to participate in your parents' plan when you are no longer a student. There are, however a number of options you should be aware of that will provide health coverage until you find permanent employment and qualify to participate in your employer's health plan. The most important thing to remember is that you will need some form of health insurance as soon as you leave college.

If you decide to sign up at a temp agency after graduation, you should know that an increasing number of temp agencies are offering some form of health insurance to those who work for them. If you sign up with several agencies, it's a good idea to inquire about whether they offer a health insurance plan.

Most large insurance companies offer short-term "transition insurance" policies that cover an individual for one to six months and can be renewed for one additional short-term period. The coverage is adequate, and the terms of the insurance are not unlike long-term policies. The cost of the typical transition policy depends upon the dollar amount allowed as deductible. Those policies which have a larger deductible (say, $500), cost about $300 for a period of six months. If you choose a plan with a $100 deductible, your premium will be considerably higher. Unlike automobile insurance, where men pay higher premiums than women, the premium for women is higher because of the possibility of pregnancy. On the positive side, transition insurance does give you good, short-term protection with a major insurer. My children chose to go this route when they graduated and did not yet have a job that offered health insurance.

Health Maintenance Organizations (HMOs) offer insurance that provides good health coverage and, in most cases, is cheaper than the comprehensive coverage of an organization such as Blue Cross (see sidebar on following page). You may want to check out various HMOs with co-workers, your new neighbors, or friends who have lived in your city for a while. Some HMOs have a better reputation than others, and it's worthwhile to investigate the companies as well as the plans offered.

The law known as COBRA (Consolidated Omnibus Budget Reconciliation Act of 1985) is directed at private health insurance coverage. One of the clauses of this law states that "the continuation of benefits for 36 months must be offered to a dependent child who loses eligibility under the generally applicable requirements of the plan." Essentially, this means that you can still be insured under a parent's employer's plan, but now you will have to pay the employer for that insurance on a monthly basis.

TUTORIAL: HEALTH INSURANCE TERMS

Confused about the different types of health insurance policies? Read the descriptions below for help:

Indemnity (Fee-for-Service): "Traditional" plan that allows you to go to any hospital or doctor. You submit a claim and pay the invoice (to be reimbursed later), or authorize the hospital or doctor to collect their fees directly from your insurance company. Very flexible in who provides your care. Higher premiums than in other types of health insurance. Coverage usually not provided until deductible has been satisfied.

PPO (Preferred Provider Organization): Insurance company has a network of "preferred providers" (hospitals, doctors, clinics, etcetera) who discount their service fees in exchange for being part of the network. Penalty for going outside the network: you'll have to submit a claim and pay a higher deductible. Cheaper than, but not as flexible as, the indemnity plan.

HMO (Health Maintenance Organization): *All* your medical services are provided by the organization's doctors, hospitals, etcetera. Much like a strict PPO: You *must* use the providers they authorize (except for emergencies as defined by your plan). Your doctor refers you to other doctors within the HMO as necessary. No deductibles. Usually requires only small copayment for each service. May also be a maximum to what you pay annually "out-of-pocket."

POS (Point-Of-Service): An option of the HMO, with greater flexibility. Your primary doctor may refer you to someone outside of the HMO with minimal or no additional cost. You may also refer yourself to a non-HMO provider, but you'll have to pay coinsurance.

It's probably a good idea to talk with your parents or another relative about the options available to you. Remember, in most cases, these plans will be only temporary, stopgap measures until you join a plan provided by your employer.

Suppose your health plan does allow you to choose your own doctor. How do you go about finding someone who is competent and easy to talk to? Your state's medical society has listings of primary care physicians as well as specialists in all fields. Also, physician referral services are offered by most hospitals. Again, ask neighbors, friends, family, and co-workers how they like their physicians. Don't hesitate to call or visit a local hospital to obtain a list of doctors who are on the staff. The local Visiting Nurses Association (www.vnaa.org) may be willing to make specific recommendations, as well.

You may choose to visit a local clinic instead of a physician in private practice. Fees in most clinics are usually adjusted to your ability to pay. Most doctors donate a specified number of hours to clinic practice, and the quality of care is often excellent.

Sometimes leaving college and encountering change in every aspect of your life cause feelings of being overwhelmed and alone. It is not unusual for people who are in the midst of making so many choices in their lives to seek counseling. Talking to a professional about the pressing issues you are facing can make your transitions less stressful.

If you find that you are not sleeping well, feeling out of control frequently, and at the same time are having difficulty in your relationships with friends, co-workers, and family, you probably should talk to a professional. Once again, friends are a good source for referrals. Even if you are now living in another part of the country, your college counseling center can provide you with a list of licensed therapists or counselors in your area. Also, the American Psychological Association (www.apa.org) will give you information and supply you with names of people you can consult.

HEALTHCARE on the Web

Comprehensive sites

The Internet houses a wealth of information on medical conditions, health insurance, drugs and medications, alternative medicine, fitness issues, and much more. Use a search engine to quickly sort through hundreds of Web sites in dozens of health categories, or start with one of these helpful sites:

www.aol.com/webcenters/health   www.webmd.com

health.yahoo.com   www.onhealth.com

www.intelihealth.com   healthwatch.medscape.com

Find a doctor

If you've moved to a new city, you'll need to find a doctor at some point. While the Internet does contain several "doctor finder" directories, you might be worried about the quality of care you'll get from doctors you know nothing about. Your best bet is the American Medical Association's searchable directory at **www.ama-assn.org**: It allows you to search by name, city or zip code, and medical specialty, and provides info on virtually every licensed physician in the U.S., including their *verified* academic and professional credentials as well as personal practice profiles.

Fill a prescription

Sites such as **www.drugstore.com** let you get your prescriptions online (no, your computer won't start spitting out pills from its disk drive!). Just have your doctor call in the prescription, or enter your info online to have their staff contact your doctor or current pharmacy, and you'll receive the meds in the mail within a few days. Not the best option for those unexpected illnesses, but great for refilling any regularly prescribed medication—you'll even get an e-mail reminder whenever their records show that your prescription is running low.

Paying for counseling doesn't necessarily have to be a problem. Most insurance plans have at least some mental health benefits. The fees at clinics can range from $20 to $50 per session, depending on the circumstances. Often, group therapy—which is considerably less expensive—can be very helpful. Your parents might help you with the payments if needed. No matter what type of counseling you choose, there are two important things to remember. One is to choose a licensed mental health professional with an

M.D., Ph.D., Ed.D., or an M.S.W. degree. The second is not to procrastinate: If you think you need to talk to someone, just go!

Keeping good records of your medical and pharmaceutical expenses is very important. Make sure to ask for receipts when you write a check or pay cash for your office visit. In some cases, you will need to present those receipts to the insurance company in order to be reimbursed, and you will certainly want to be repaid!

EMPLOYER BENEFITS

When you reach the point where you are considering a job offer, you should pay careful attention to all the benefits offered by the employer. The average cost to an employer for providing benefits is between 25 and 30 percent of the employee's salary. This benefit, along with the ones mentioned below, is considered part of your salary package.

Retirement Plans: Most employers offer some sort of retirement plan such as a 401(k), which allows you to put a percentage of your pretax income into an investment fund. In a good many cases employers will match your contribution and add to your investment. If you change jobs, you can take your retirement accumulations with you.

Employee Assistance Program (EAP): These programs deal with providing counseling to help the employee in order to resolve concerns dealing with issues such as marital or relationship problems, substance abuse, or any issues that may affect your job performance.

Tuition reimbursement: Even though you probably would like a break from attending classes at this point, having your employer pay for all or part of your additional study is a big benefit. If your classes are related to the business of the company, the employer will probably pay all the tuition fees. In some cases, employers will reimburse you for unrelated courses as well.

PTO bank: Paid time off banks are replacing the vacation and sick days most companies offer. Instead of allocating a designated number of days for vacation and illness, the company allows you to "bank" vacation, personal, and sick days. You can then use your allotted time as you wish, which makes for greater flexibility.

Flextime: More employers are now offering employees the opportunity to vary their work hours. The usual nine-to-five workday is not suitable for everyone, and employers are allowing people to choose, within limits, alternative hours.

Telecommuting: Employers may allow (or even encourage) certain employees to work from home, either part-time or full-time. This flexible work arrangement is gaining popularity as industries become more and more dependent on the computer, cutting the need for face-to-face interaction.

These and other benefits can add thousands of dollars to your compensation package and should be carefully examined before accepting a job offer. Keep in mind that benefits are negotiable: If you choose to ask the employer for some changes in the standard benefit package you are offered, be sure to present your request in writing, detailing the changes you're requesting. Explain the reasons for your request. If, for example, you believe your employer's plan for tuition reimbursement is not a very good one, you could emphasize the fact that education should be a lifelong process, and that an employee who is better informed, and aware of current trends in a particular field, will be an asset to the company. At the same time, you should be prepared to give up a benefit that you don't need at this time—perhaps day-care services or payment for eyeglasses. Once again, your well organized thoughts and your negotiation skills can help you get a plan that meets your needs at this stage in your life.

chapter 8
YOU *CAN* GO HOME AGAIN

"When it was time for my daughter to graduate from college, she really wasn't certain about which graduate school to attend or even which degree to pursue, so I prepared for her to return to the homestead. Her college was just 40 minutes from home, so it would not be a difficult physical adjustment for Sarah. Moving home gave her the opportunity to find a full-time position, begin repaying college loans, purchase her first new car, build a bank account again, start investing in mutual funds, and generally get her feet on the ground."
—P. Deston, Parent

It's been four or five years since you lived at home, and after being on your own in college the idea of returning to your parents' place after graduation is probably the last thing on Earth you'd like to think about. Suddenly, you remember all the negative aspects of living with your parents. The arguments about your excessive use of the phone, the constant reminders about the messiness of your room, and the discussions about the late hours you kept are all too vivid in your mind. Why did this have to happen to you? And more importantly, what can you do to make sure things will be different than they were four years ago?

Let me assure you that your parents are just as leery as you about your impending return to *their* house. They, too, are remembering the days when they were unable to get near the phone because you were seemingly engaged in a constant telethon with your friends. They still shudder at the sight of your clothes piled in a heap on the floor of your room. And the thought of your getting ready to leave the house to meet your friends at 10:30—precisely the hour they are getting ready for bed—still sends

"I was lucky because I was able to move home, so housing wasn't really a problem. I hadn't lived at home for over three years, so going back to that small room after having a big apartment was a huge transition. I was no longer living like I was used to, I was living like my parents wanted me to. It meant getting up earlier to get ready for work and not being able to rest when the dinner table needed to be set, but you get used to it. My parents had to get used to me again, too. Because of financial circumstances, I still live with them, but as soon as the opportunity arises, I will be on my own again."

—K. Deckert, Class of '96

chills down their spines. Their empty nest will be full once again. How in the world will they handle it?

The major reason most new grads return home is economic. Your starting salary may just be too low to enable you to start out on your own. In some instances you soon discover that most of your salary is spent paying the rent, and you have little left for necessities like clothes, buying groceries, and going to an occasional movie with friends. Moving home may not be part of the scenario you visualized, but it can enable you to save enough money so that you can eventually have a place of your own.

Some people return home for a short time after graduation because they don't really have a clear plan of action and need time and financial assistance while they work on sorting it all out. If you are uncertain about which career direction you'd like to pursue, living at home will help ease your financial obligations and enable you to concentrate on experimenting and finding the best niche for yourself in the workplace. It will enable you to concentrate on finding your ideal job and lessen your concern about the financial burdens confronting you.

Recent surveys indicate that an increasing number of students return home after college. Some stay for a very limited time, while others stay for a year or two, or even longer. I spoke with a number of people and learned that many new graduates view the move not as a last resort, but as an opportunity to ease the pressures involved in adjusting to the next stage of their lives. Some feel it was a really good experience that enabled them to reconnect, as an adult, with their families.

Communication is one of the vital elements of any successful relationship. Good communication between you and your parents is *absolutely essential* if you are planning to return home. If your relationship with your parents has been less than fantastic in the past, it is particularly important for you to clear the air at this time and engage them in a dialogue *before* you move back home. Setting ground rules for all the people involved should be one of the first items on your agenda.

"I was filled with excitement at the prospect of seeing my 'little girl' back home after her absence. Her returns were usually filled with school work, catching up with high school and other friends, and partying whenever the opportunity presented itself. Being the optimist, I didn't have any apprehension."

—T. Deckert, Parent

You may want to "call a meeting" or perhaps buy a pizza and invite your folks to join you for lunch. It doesn't really matter how you choose to set up the talk. What's important is that you designate a time and place that will give you an opportunity to talk and to listen to each other.

You could start the conversation by introducing the realities of your current status. Indicate to your family that you have changed and grown in a number of directions since you've been away at college. You alone have been responsible for your well-being, for scheduling and keeping appointments, for taking care of matters relating to your health, for balancing your checkbook, and for doing your laundry. Try to convey to them that you have matured and have truly enjoyed

"I was concerned with how Kristen would re-adjust to living at home. Were we going to threaten her independence?"

—C. Deckert, Parent

I think the most difficult adjustment for me that first year after college was living with my parents, who had difficulty accepting the changes and independence I had acquired in college. I had to find a way of retaining my freedom and I had to conquer the fear of the unknown, since my life could take on different directions without the structure of school. For the first time, life didn't have a structure in place. It was the first time that the academic calendar didn't control my year. Furthermore, my peers started going in different directions. I had to follow my own individual path while trying to maintain ties to the past."

—B. Mecca, Class of '91

assuming these many responsibilities during the past four years. You may want to point out that you've also enjoyed the freedom your current lifestyle allows you to have, and hope you can incorporate some of that freedom when you return home.

Ask your parents how their lives have changed since you left for college and *really listen* to their responses. If you were the last child to leave home, or if your youngest sister or brother will be going off to school just when you return, your parents may have a more difficult time of it. They may have been looking forward to a quieter atmosphere in their home. Initiating this conversation and resolving issues that may trigger old reactions to certain situations will help demonstrate to your folks that you have, in fact, matured. It's important that you try to set rules and maintain boundaries now!

Recent grads who have returned home suggest that a good starting point for this meeting is for both parties—you and your parents—to compile a "bug" list. What kinds of situations bugged you most when you lived at home? Was it the strict curfews, the constant reminder to straighten your room, or the unasked for comments about your friends? In some cases it may have been all of the above. At the same time you're listing your gripes, ask your parents to jot down which of your habits were most annoying to them. Were you frequently late for meals? Did your friends become permanent fixtures in your house? Did you have to be constantly reminded that the volume of the music you were listening to was disturbing others in the household?

These issues, stated on paper, should be the starting point for the contract you and your parents will negotiate. As with all negotiations, you will need to stay calm, stick to the issues involved, and stand your ground. It's always a good idea to remember to use *I* statements when discussing a particular issue about which you feel strongly. It's usually more effective to say "*I* really have a difficult time dealing with . . . ." than to accusingly state "You always expect me to . . ." If your goal is to be treated as an equal, it's important that you not revert to the somewhat childish behavior patterns you may have displayed in the past.

After you've had the initial conversation, it's a good idea to compile a comprehensive list of issues that will be included in the contract. What expectations and apprehensions do your parents have at this time? What kinds of behavior and support would you like them to exhibit towards you? Mention that neither you nor they are the same people you were before you left for college. You've all grown in a number of areas and in separate directions. Talk honestly about how you have changed, and how apprehensive you are about reverting to the same negative aspects of your precollege relationship with your folks. Clearly, there are many issues involved in everyone's expectations. Every family has its own unique situations and hangups to deal with. *Engaging in dialogue, and really listening to your parents' concerns are essential elements of a successful transition.* Acknowledging the growth and changes experienced by everyone during these past few years is a necessary component of that dialogue, It really is possible to establish a healthy relationship built on trust and good communication. As with building other relationships, it takes time and hard work.

85

"The thought of adjusting to living with my family again frightened me. Emotionally, I was down about not finding work, and returning home would be an added stress. Later on, after living at home for a while, I realized that my family was a constant source of support!"

—M. Vieira, Class of '94

"Two of my children returned home after finishing college. I was a little apprehensive to have them return because I knew that they had become quite independent and might resent any restrictions I might place on them. I thought about what my values were and what I would find unacceptable behavior. It seemed that it all boiled down to respect and good manners."

—C. DiPrete, Parent

CONTRACTUAL AGREEMENT WITH PARENTS

You may want to use some of the issues described below as a guideline for your own discussion with your folks. These areas were suggested by recent grads who returned home shortly after leaving school and who did, in fact, draw up contractual agreements with their parents. How many of these issues are relevant to your situation? What specific steps do you need to take in order to resolve some of the anticipated problems? How are you going to start? When are you going to take the first step? At any rate, here's the list. Look over the issues mentioned and include any items that you think may be problematic for you in your list of issues to discuss with your parents.

CURFEWS

At school you could stay out as late as you wanted. Now you have to address the expectations of your parents, and if there's one common quality that all parents share when it comes to their sons and daughters, it's that *parents worry a lot.* Let them know that you are aware of their concern for your safety and reinforce the fact that you are a sensible adult who has lived responsibly during the time you were away at school. Keeping them informed of your plans is a good idea. Let them know that you expect to be out very late, without stating a specific time of return. If, however, you have told them that you expect to be home by 1:00, and find later that your plans have changed, it's important that you phone and inform your parents, or leave a message letting them know you'll be home later than you had anticipated. It's important, too, that you let them know in advance if you plan not to be home at all for the night.

FINANCES

Do your parents expect you to pay rent or perhaps contribute money towards the purchase of groceries, or are they willing and able to have you live at home without making a monetary contribution to the household? Your parents need to be clear about this. If you think their demands are unreasonable, perhaps you can negotiate, and help them out by performing special chores in lieu of contributing money. The important factor here is to have an honest discussion about their expectations of you.

THE TELEPHONE

Telephone use and abuse usually ranks as one of the major areas of conflict between students returning home and their parents. It is vital that "telephone rules" be established before you move in. At college, sharing newsworthy events with your friends was easy: You either visited their dorm room or used the phone (probably located in or near your room) to fill them in on all the exciting happenings. Once you're living at home, even if you have your own phone extension in your room, you will need to be aware of other members of the household who may be waiting to make or receive calls. Paying for the long-distance calls you make is an issue that should be discussed. Being aware of talking for reasonable amounts of time is essential too. When my daughter returned home, she immediately contacted the phone company and had her own line installed because she realized that I have a fairly low tolerance for phone abuse. She lived at home for almost three years, and I am convinced her foresight helped us avoid hundreds of arguments.

"The biggest concerns we had after our daughter returned home related to economic issues such as continuing health insurance and automobile expenses. Our hope was that she would be able to land a job within six months that provided full medical benefits and a decent salary. This would allow her to purchase an automobile and enjoy independent living. Secondarily, we had some apprehension about resuming consideration of her in our daily plans, such as making sure we were home at meal times."

—T. Carroll, Parent

87

"I was apprehensive about the fact that my daughter had not had any restrictions or curfews while at college. What was it going to be like now that she was at home? Would she expect that same freedom? Would I be up late at night waiting for her to come home? Could I lay down the rules? These questions always ran through my mind."

—J. Rego, Parent

RESPONSIBILITIES AND DUTIES

You're moving back home and will once again become part of that household, if only for a limited period of time. It's important to talk about issues such as meals, household duties, etcetera. Do you want to take care of your own laundry, or can another member of the household do it? (This, by the way, is an area mentioned by a good many grads as being fertile ground for arguments). Do you want to have sole responsibility for straightening your room, or would you welcome someone else vacuuming or making up your bed? It's important to think ahead and determine the day-to-day responsibilities you'd like to assume.

At the same time, you need to know what your parents' expectations are. Which chores dealing with ordinary maintenance of the house will you be expected to do? Are gardening, cutting the grass, shoveling snow, washing windows, or babysitting (if you have younger siblings) expected of you? If both parents work, and you have a part-time job, will you be expected to lend a hand with meal preparations? Of course, it goes without saying that if there's a huge snowstorm, you'll help out without being asked. You'll need to determine which duties you'll be expected to perform routinely. Again, if you believe your parents' expectations are unreasonable, let them know how you feel.

ENTERTAINING FRIENDS

If I were to rank areas of possible disagreement, the issue of friends—specifically the sleeping arrangements for friends of the opposite sex—would certainly be near the top of the list. How do your parents feel about your boyfriend or girlfriend sleeping over? Most parents welcome friends, but some will insist that he or she sleep in a room other than yours. Others feel comfortable allowing you to choose the sleeping arrangements. When you talk with your parents, handle this topic with sensitivity and tact.

The frequency and number of visitors you have may also be an issue. So much depends upon the size of your parents' home: It may be difficult for your college friends to visit for the weekend if your folks live in a small apartment. The logistics of such a visit would need careful planning. Some parents prefer to take off and spend time visiting their friends or relatives when their children's friends come to visit.

> "The most difficult aspect of our readjustment concerned household situations—more clutter, increased phone calls. I found myself worrying about where she was going, and what time she would be home."
>
> —C. Deckert, Parent

MEALTIME TOGETHERNESS

89

"Once my children returned, we had a long talk about expectations. One of them had expected me to resume the role of mother, which meant cooking the meals, doing the laundry, cleaning the house, etcetera. After one or two encounters when I came home after working and was asked what we were having for dinner, I made it clear that I was no longer responsible for her daily care, especially since she was not working. At that point, I told her that as long as she was unemployed, she would be expected to do some of the daily chores in the house and that I expected her to be actively pursuing employment. She soon became employed. However, I did expect both of them to participate in the daily functioning of the house, even if they were employed."
—C. DiPrete, Parent

Do your parents expect you to be present at meals? If the family usually has dinner at 6:30 or 7:00, will you be expected to dine with them? If that arrangement is mutually acceptable, then it is your responsibility to let them know that you will be late, or perhaps not present at all, for dinner. If, however, you feel uncomfortable with the structure of that arrangement,

"Finding a job and moving back in with my parents were probably the two biggest and most difficult adjustments I had to make. I was still scanning the classifieds daily, trying to figure out how I would ever regain the sense of independence that I had for the last four years. I lived at home for the next year and a half, working for a local newspaper. It was something to put spending money into my pocket while I feverishly searched for something more closely related to my field of interest. I finally landed a job that interested me enough to relocate to the Boston area. I shared an apartment with a friend and knew I was finally on my way to leaving Mom and Dad's comfortable nest."

—M. Tartaglione, Class of '94

tell your folks that you would prefer to be responsible for getting your own meal at dinnertime. It might be a good idea for them never to expect you for dinner unless you let them know in advance that you'll be there.

When you sit down and talk with your parents about reentering the family home, it might be a good idea to invoke the "friends" rule—treating each other in the same manner as you would treat a good friend. How would Mom or Dad react if one of their friends arrived late for a meal? What would you do if you were headed to a friend's house for dinner and realized that you couldn't possibly be on time, that you would probably be at least a half hour late? A good many arguments can be avoided if everyone involved makes a conscious effort to utilize the "friends" rule often, and particularly in potentially volatile situations.

It may take a little bit of time to readjust to the rhythms of your childhood home. As with other changes in our lives, being aware of the rules and expectations helps. I can assure you that when you are ready to move into a place of your own, you will probably miss some of the benefits you enjoyed while living with your parents.

chapter 9
FRIENDS ARE FOREVER

In the introduction to this book, I talked about some of the behavioral aspects of seniors who really don't want to deal with saying goodbye to the close friends they've made during the past four years. The prospect of leaving their wonderful college experience behind brings much sadness to most students. Time and again, as I talked with seniors, they would declare that these past few years have been the "best years of my life." In a way, the dire need for graduating seniors to talk about and deal with their feelings was responsible for my Reality 101 course in the first place. There is little doubt that your college friends have become your family. You have shared good and bad times with them, and have spent thousands of hours together during the past four or five years. You would be truly unusual if you didn't feel a great sadness at this time.

As you become ready to move on to the next stage of your life, look back and re-examine your own style of dealing with changes in your past. Have passages and transitions in your life been hard for you? Was the transition to middle school difficult for you? Did it take you a long time to adjust to the new teachers? Were you overwhelmed when you finally reached high school? Was being at the bottom of the barrel once again scary for you? Was leaving home for college a traumatic experience? Can you identify how you dealt with your feelings? What worked for you then?

Perhaps you've noticed that the patterns of change in the life of a student have been pretty consistent; they progress from being at the very bottom of the ladder and eventually work their way up to the top rung. Each time you get to the top, or graduate, you start over again at the bottom. Now, as you're about to leave college and once again find yourself on the

"If anyone asked me about friendships after college, I would say exactly the same thing I was told by an alum—that you will keep your friends, but that things will be different. My college friends and I have maintained close friendships, but it takes a little effort and planning to get together."

—M. P. Burke, Class of '92

bottom rung, it's important to remember that it's just a matter of time before you start your ascent. The arena has changed, but the process is very much the same.

GRADUATION DAY

Graduation day is worrisome for many students and a hurdle they'd like to overcome. Not only does that particular event signal the official end of your student days, but it may present potentially unpleasant situations involving your family. Many people whose divorced parents do not communicate well dread the thought of family confrontations on that occasion. It helps to be proactive, and talk to your parents about *your* hopes and expectations for your special day. Think about how you would like to facilitate this day and share your thoughts with them. If you have older siblings who have gone through graduation, try to determine which familial strategies worked well and which you'd like to avoid. Perhaps your sister or brother could suggest a workable plan of action for a pleasant, appropriate celebration after the graduation ceremony is over. In almost all cases, family members are very much aware of how important this day is to you and will try hard to be cooperative. It's important, however, that you communicate your wishes to them.

SAYING GOODBYE

After spending many years listening to the concerns of college seniors, I truly believe that of all the issues they are dealing with, the most emotional is separation from their friends. I have asked Kathie Oliveira, a career counseling colleague and facilitator of the Reality 101 program, to share some of her thoughts on this subject.

"The most poignant moments in my Reality 101 sessions happened on the days we covered saying goodbye and going home. Although I vividly remember the emotions that I experienced when I graduated from college many years ago, the depth of the emotion has faded over time. For students actually going through the experience, the fear of losing their friends is overwhelming.

"College is a time when students come into their own. Away from home for the first time, they make new friends, learn about others from different places and cultures, experience the freedom of making their own decisions, and share disappointments, successes, heartbreak and happiness . . . life. At any given time of the day or night, a student can cross the hall and have a friend there immediately. Students hate to go home for vacations and the summer because these friends will be far away. Suddenly it is senior year, and they realize that this lifestyle is about to end.

"For many students the anxiety of leaving actually results in physical symptoms. 'I get up in the morning, and I just can't get going. I can't think, I don't feel like eating, and I don't have the energy to do anything.' Many students talk about just not feeling like themselves. Others become moody, and exhibit symptoms that are depression-like in nature. Still others don't say anything, but their actions speak louder than words. They start skipping classes, thinking that if they flunk out, they'll be able to stay longer. Some start partying more, while some pull back and lose all contact with their friends. 'If I'm going to leave them anyway, I might as well get it over with now, then it won't hurt as much.'

"Leaving and the sadness it brings are part of life. Expect it, but also remember back four years to when you graduated from high school. You were leaving all of those friends and memories behind. And yet, you found ways to stay in touch with those people who meant the most to you.

"The same is true for college friends. Some will always be there and some will become less involved in your life along the way. Your true friends will always be with you. While your get-togethers may be different and more spread apart, they will still be there, and those connections will become stronger as you share yet another phase of your lives with each other."

ALUMNI SERVICES on the Web

It's easy to stay in touch with former classmates and favorite faculty members over the Internet. During that last week before graduation, start collecting e-mail addresses (and snail-mail addresses, too, while you're at it!) of people you'd like to hear from. Don't wait until Graduation Day—there will be *way* too much going on and you'll end up going home without any addresses at all!

Another way to keep yourself informed about what's going on with your fellow alums is to visit your school's Web site. You'll find links to the Office of Alumni Services, as well as the Career Services Office, which can be extremely helpful in finding job leads and contact information.

You don't even need to confine yourself to your own alma mater. Use resources from *other* schools by checking out *their* Web sites—often, you'll find that their career and alumni services are available to everybody. Comprehensive lists of university Alumni Offices can be found at **www.rpi.edu/dept/cdc/alumni/**, and university Career Services Offices at **www.rpi.edu/dept/cdc/carserv/**.

94

STAYING IN TOUCH

Now you are going to leave the friends with whom you have spent the last four years sharing your joys, your disappointments and your dreams. You keep saying nothing will change once you graduate, but deep inside you know it just won't be the same. You are absolutely right: It won't be the same, *but the friendships will last and grow for many years to come.* It will take some effort, but good friendships continue to blossom throughout life despite frequent geographical changes. We all know people who have maintained close contact with their college friends throughout the years. Each summer, I go hiking with several women whom I have known since elementary school. We live in different parts of the country, but we have managed to meet each year and continue our close friendship. You might want to plan a series of get-togethers as soon as possible, so that you know, before you leave school, the next time you will be seeing each other.

chapter 10

THE WORDS OF THE
PARENTS AND THE GRADS

As I started to write *Reality 101*, it occurred to me that people who had graduated within the last seven or eight years might like to share some of their experiences and insights with those students who are about to step out into the world beyond the college campus.

I've asked Reality 101 graduates to respond to four questions for this section:

- As a senior, what aspects of leaving college were most frightening to you?
- In retrospect, what was the most difficult adjustment for you that first year after college?
- How have your priorities changed since you left college?
- What advice would you give to seniors, about to enter the work place at the end of the twentieth century?

Their responses to the first two questions are interspersed throughout the book, but I thought it might be more helpful to present their parting thoughts dealing with their current priorities and their advice to new grads in the closing chapter.

Several months after I started writing, I also began to wonder about the parents of the grads who had returned home. What were the issues about which *they* felt strongly? Were their reactions to their child's return pretty much the same as their son's and daughter's? What advice would they offer to parents now facing that same transition? I contacted a number of people, asking essentially the same questions the alumni and alumnae had answered. Let's listen to the parents first, and then continue the dialogue with the voices of the grads.

PARENTS' RESPONSE AND ADVICE

"I still have a hard time dealing with four adults in our home as opposed to two adults and two children. I realize that my children are now adults, have minds of their own, and have the right to make their own decisions, but when their priorities differ from mine, it takes a while to accept their very fragile independence (they don't pay rent). I also didn't expect all of the complications to our routine household schedule: The basic morning problem of who gets the bathroom and when is intensified because we all depend on the right timing to perform well at work."

"Strongly offered opinions for the 'good' of our daughter were usually rejected out of hand. These were usually what I thought were 'best' for her career. In retrospect, I see that I was talking down to a child and not to an adult with those opinions. It was very difficult remembering my little girl was an adult, and today's job market is quite different from when I got my first job."

"Asking nonintrusive questions regarding career choices, finances, and future plans worked best. The questions were answered with additional data when they were nonthreatening and supportive in nature. Standard rules of the home still applied and were accepted; surprisingly, they were about the same that were enforced by Kristen as a resident assistant."

"As far as advice for parents is concerned, we would suggest that they attempt to give the new graduate as much independence for decision making as can be tolerated. Try to be more of a listener and a helpmate in their job pursuits. Be sensitive to the stress that new graduates are under to find a decent job and establish economic independence despite the fact that they mask that stress. Don't let your anxiety over inadequate job search techniques show through. In other words, be suggestive but not critical in discussing your son or daughter's job-hunting techniques or lack thereof."

"The most difficult aspect of my readjustment was the messy bathroom and her messy bedroom. I finally said it was not worth nagging her about the room: I would just close the door to her bedroom so I wouldn't have

to look at it. As far as the bathroom was concerned, I threatened to throw everything out the window if she didn't clean up after herself."

"After she was home everything worked itself into place and it really was not a problem. However, I did place some restrictions as far as not coming home at a ridiculous hour is concerned. She was to call if she was delayed, or if something happened. I told her these were the rules and that she would have to abide by them if she was going to continue to live at home. I did find her to be more mature and more reasonable at this point."

"I would advise parents to enjoy having their children back home. This time will pass and you will soon be faced with an empty nest."

"I tried to avoid confrontations and meddling in her affairs. Asking too many questions and telling her that she comes in too late at night did not work well. I tried hard not to threaten the independence she developed, but yet make sure she abided by house rules."

"Be careful how you relate to your child. Remember that they are adults now. Remember how you acted and reacted when you were in their shoes."

"The rules I set up were that they could not have opposite-sex guests sleep over. However, they were not obliged to be home every night. On the other hand, if they were not going to be home for meals or for the night, I should be informed as a courtesy. And I should do the same for them if I was not going to be home—it worked both ways. I also expected them to pay their own expenses for entertainment, clothing, long distance phone bills, dry cleaning bills—anything that had to do with them specifically. I also expected them to buy some groceries once they were employed. I did not charge them rent."

"I didn't expect them to tell me everything, only what they wished to. I very much respected their privacy and they respected mine. I was there as a mother, but not in a controlling way."

"All in all, we worked out a good living arrangement with both girls and they became very responsible about letting me know when they were

going to be home, etcetera. They have now moved on in their lives, and we are very good 'friends.' That grew out of respect for one another."

"Life is constantly changing, causing human beings to change along with it. Sarah's needs have changed, and so our relationship has brought us more on an even par with one another as adults. I must be careful not to treat her as my little daughter when the situation calls for an adult relationship. Sometimes I win, sometimes I lose!

"It is almost three years now, and Sarah is ready to move on to an apartment of her own. She would like a place to call her own so that she can be responsible for the finances and all the chores that accompany having her own apartment. She would like to be able to entertain her friends in her own place and on her own terms.

"It is very important to encourage their growth as they need to know you support their independence. I believe they need to leave the nest and fly on their own as soon as possible, for their own sense of accomplishment. However, they need to be in a financial situation that allows them to take care of themselves. Sarah has reached that point now."

"Treat your returning son or daughter as you would a respected friend. Respect their opinions and offer unrequested advice sparingly!"

ADVICE FROM THE GRADS

Now let's look at the grads' responses to how their priorities have changed since they left college and what advice they'd like to offer to new graduates.

On Changing Priorities

"I think my priorities have changed very much since I left college. I believe that my attitude played a strong role in that change. Before I graduated, I had many ideas of what life would be like after college.

"I thought that having a college degree would guarantee me a job—one with good benefits, a great salary, and a great working environment. In

theory, it all seemed perfect. But it is not always like that. Because I had such high expectations, I was saddened and discouraged when I opened the want ads. Anyway, I now realize that I am lucky to have a job and believe that hard work, my health, family, and friends, are the most important things in my life."

"My priorities have definitely changed since I graduated from college. I used to think moving up within a corporation would make me happy, that my career would always come first. After working long hours and weekends, I realize that this type of life is not for me. I value being with friends and family more than money and prestige. I have also learned caring for family gives more pleasure than working."

"I now think more about the future and stability (financial more than emotional). I worry about money and furthering my career, and I often wonder if I'm in the right field and doing the right job for me."

"Since I have left college, my priorities have changed immensely. Three years ago my priorities were studying for exams and maintaining a decent G.P.A. Now my priorities are career and money related. I am striving to make important and positive contributions to my place of employment, as well as establish a solid financial background for myself. Instead of speaking with career counselors, I am now speaking with realtors and mortgage consultants. How things change!"

"My priorities have basically remained the same. I'm not married and don't have children. I have, however, realized that every step taken in my career is a means of self-improvement, so I am consistently trying to succeed and better myself."

"I think that my priorities have definitely changed. When I graduated, I was intrigued by the thought of "Corporate America." Having an expense account, wearing suits to work, doing business lunches, and traveling seemed like the ultimate life for a career-oriented woman. I have worked for a Fortune 500 company for three years now, and I have recently begun to realize that I sacrificed a lot of 'me' for my job. I sit at a desk for the better part of the day and sometimes don't get to see the

light of day. I no longer have time to write and draw and 'play' like I always made time for. It suddenly doesn't seem as appealing as it once was. On the other hand, I have worked very hard and have seen the rewards of my dedication."

"My priorities have changed a lot. I no longer worry about being able to go to the biggest party of the year; I worry about getting enough sleep so I can go to work. I no longer spend hours on the phone because I have too much to do before getting to work. When I feel lousy in the morning, I can't skip that 9:00 A.M. meeting. I also used to drop everything for my friends, but now I have to put things off because I'm too busy. The days are longer and the naps are few and far between. I guess this is why they call it reality, and not one big party like college."

Advice to New Grads

"My youngest brother graduated from college in May, and I would offer seniors the same advice I gave him. Get a taste of the real world by taking on an internship. This will help you see what goes on in companies, law firms, hospitals, etcetera. It also helps you to get accustomed to working with people of all ages, nationalities, cultures, and anybody else that may not resemble a college student. Even if you don't know what you want to get into, you can always find out later. Continue to work hard and do not get discouraged. Even if you need to start at the bottom in a company, work hard, learn all you can, and be indispensable. At the same time, keep thinking about what else you might like to do."

"As to my advice for graduating seniors, I say enjoy it while it lasts. After you're out, you will miss everything—even late-night cramming for exams, and all of those little tests, papers, and projects you stressed over will seem so obsolete. I strongly recommend applying for internships. The experience you gain is worth so much more than grades. The people you meet will soon be your colleagues or maybe even contacts. But remember that all your hard work will eventually pay off!"

"Seniors should pursue graduate work to make them more competitive in the marketplace and develop their intellect further in order to set themselves apart from others."

"*Real life is hard work! Don't get me wrong: Being an adult has its advantages, but I've realized that I am responsible for my own happiness. The decisions I make, both good and bad, have a direct affect on my life and happiness.*"

"*Be patient. Things have a way of working out. But that doesn't mean not trying, and waiting for things just to happen. You must be aggressive and persevere. You must not take it to heart when yet another rejection letter finds its way to your mailbox. You must look adversity in the face and challenge it. Accept it as an invitation to work and try harder, and then things will begin to happen. For some it might take two years after graduation, while others might succeed in two months. Take that first job out of college, whatever it might be, and do the best you can at it. Take it seriously, and don't give up. Find a way to do what you want to do. It won't happen overnight, but eventually something will come up. And don't be afraid to be afraid! It's okay. And believe me, as you will see for yourself, it's really not that bad. There are worse things that can happen. Good luck!*"

"*My advice would be to take baby steps—don't expect too much too fast. It's amazing, if you're patient, everything has a way of falling into place. It's very important to feel success in one's own mind, no matter what you do.*"

"*My main advice would be to never give up! You can accomplish all of your goals, be whatever you want to be, and go as far as you want to go. You just have to want it badly enough. The old saying comes into play here, 'You can do anything you set your mind to!' Also, don't be afraid to fail. It happens to the best of us and if used as a learning device, it will only make you stronger and more determined. Everyone makes mistakes, but we learn from them. Those who dwell on mistakes live for the past, while those who learn from their mistakes create the future. And most importantly: Life is short, have fun!*"

"*The advice I would give to seniors is to really know yourself. Know what your heart wants and follow it, because doing what you love and being with people you trust, like family and close friends, will make you*" *happy in your career and in life. Just follow your instincts and intuition and you will never go wrong."*

"When I was in college my priorities were friends and school, in that order. However, after being out of college for a couple of years, my priorities have changed, to include marriage, work, family, school, and friends. In just listing my priorities, I am amazed at how simple life was in college. Once you get out into the 'real world' your responsibilities increase. I look back at my college years as the best years in my life. However, the last five years out of school have been my most productive and challenging. I talk to my friends, and they seem to feel the same way. These years can be difficult. We are struggling to find our purpose and direction. We are so familiar with school because we spend our lives in the classroom until the day we graduate. Then it's like, what now? We always had each year planned, until college graduation. Reality 101 addressed a number of these issues, and made it acceptable to discuss our fears. This helped us plan and take action towards our future. For me, these past five years after college have been a period of tremendous growth. I am grateful for my college experience because it gave me confidence in myself. My advice to graduating seniors is to develop a plan of action and get as much job experience as possible. Most importantly, they should believe in themselves, no matter what happens. It may be a struggle at first, but each struggle that is overcome will make you stronger!"

There's little more that I can add to the wisdom expressed by these productive, mature adults, except to say that everyone leaving college must experience and "pass" Reality 101 before they become eligible for 102! Good luck.

NOTES

NOTES

NOTES

NOTES

How Did We Do? Grade Us.

Thank you for choosing a Kaplan book. Your comments and suggestions are very useful to us. Please answer the following questions to assist us in our continued development of high-quality resources to meet your needs.

The Kaplan book I read was: _____

My name is: _____

My address is: _____

_____

My e-mail address is: _____

What overall grade would you give this book?   Ⓐ Ⓑ Ⓒ Ⓓ Ⓕ

How relevant was the information to your goals?   Ⓐ Ⓑ Ⓒ Ⓓ Ⓕ

How comprehensive was the information in this book?   Ⓐ Ⓑ Ⓒ Ⓓ Ⓕ

How accurate was the information in this book?   Ⓐ Ⓑ Ⓒ Ⓓ Ⓕ

How easy was the book to use?   Ⓐ Ⓑ Ⓒ Ⓓ Ⓕ

How appealing was the book's design?   Ⓐ Ⓑ Ⓒ Ⓓ Ⓕ

What were the book's strong points? _____

How could this book be improved? _____

Is there anything that we left out that you wanted to know more about?

Would you recommend this book to others?   ☐ YES   ☐ NO

Other comments: _____

_____

_____

Do we have permission to quote you?   ☐ YES   ☐ NO

Thank you for your help. Please tear out this page and mail it to:

Dave Chipps, Managing Editor
Kaplan Educational Centers
888 Seventh Avenue
New York, NY 10106

Or, you can answer these questions online at www.kaplan.com/talkback.

Thanks!

Want more information about our services, products, or the nearest Kaplan center?

 Call our nationwide toll-free numbers:

1-800-KAP-TEST for information on our courses, private tutoring and admissions consulting
1-800-KAP-ITEM for information on our books and software
1-888-KAP-LOAN* for information on student loans

Connect with us in cyberspace:

On AOL, keyword:"Kaplan"
On the World Wide Web, go to:
1. www.kaplan.com
2. www.kaptest.com
3. www.eSCORE.com
4. www.dearborn.com
5. www.BrassRing.com
6. www.concord.kaplan.edu
7. www.kaplancollege.com
Via e-mail: info@kaplan.com

 **Write to:**

Kaplan Educational Centers
888 Seventh Avenue
New York, NY 10106

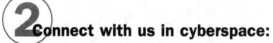

About

KAPLAN

Educational Centers

Kaplan Educational Centers is one of the nation's leading providers of education and career services. Kaplan is a wholly owned subsidiary of The Washington Post Company.

TEST PREPARATION & ADMISSIONS

Kaplan's nationally recognized test prep courses cover more than 20 standardized tests, including secondary school, college and graduate school entrance exams and foreign language and professional licensing exams. In addition, Kaplan offers private tutoring and comprehensive, one-to-one admissions and application advice for students applying to college and graduate programs. Kaplan also provides information and guidance on the financial aid process. Students can enroll in online test prep courses and admissions consulting services at www.kaptest.com

SCORE! EDUCATIONAL CENTERS

SCORE! after-school learning centers help K-9 students build confidence, academic and goal-setting skills in a motivating, sports-oriented environment. Its cutting-edge, interactive curriculum continually assesses and adapts to each child's academic needs and learning style. Enthusiastic Academic Coaches serve as positive role models, creating a high-energy atmosphere where learning is exciting and fun. *SCORE!* Prep provides in-home, one-on-one tutoring for high school academic subjects and standardized tests. www.eSCORE.com provides customized online educational resources and services for parents and kids ages 0 to 18. eSCORE.com creates a deep, evolving profile for each child based on his or her age, interests and skills. Parents can access personalized information and resources designed to help their children realize their full potential.

KAPLAN LEARNING SERVICES

Kaplan Learning Services provides customized assessment, education and professional development programs to K-12 schools and universities.

KAPLAN INTERNATIONAL PROGRAMS

Kaplan services international students and professionals in the U.S. through a series of intensive English language and test preparation programs. These programs are offered campus-based centers across the USA. Kaplan offers specialized services including housing, placement at top American universities, fellowship management, academic monitoring and reporting, and financial administration.

KAPLAN PUBLISHING

Kaplan Publishing produces books and software. Kaplan Books, a joint imprint with Simon & Schuster, publishes titles in test preparation, admissions, education, career development and life skills; Kaplan and Newsweek jointly publish guides on getting into college, finding the right career, and helping your child succeed in school. Through an alliance with Knowledge Adventure, Kaplan publishes educational software for the K-12 retail and school markets.

KAPLAN PROFESSIONAL

Kaplan Professional provides assessment, training, and certification services for corporate clients and individuals seeking to advance their careers. Member units include Dearborn, a leading supplier of licensing training and continuing education for securities, real estate, and insurance professionals; Perfect Access/CRN, which delivers software education and consultation for law firms and businesses; and Kaplan Professional Call Center Services, a total provider of services for the call center industry.

DISTANCE LEARNING DIVISION

Kaplan's distance learning programs include Concord School of Law, the nation's first online law school; and Kaplan College, a leading provider of degree and certificate programs in criminal justice and paralegal studies.

COMMUNITY OUTREACH

Kaplan provides educational career resources to thousands of financially disadvantaged students annually, working closely with educational institutions, not-for-profit groups, government agencies and other grass roots organizations on a variety of national and local support programs. Kaplan enriches local communities by employing high school, college and graduate students, creating valuable work experiences for vast numbers of young people each year.

BRASSRING

BrassRing Inc., headquartered in New York and San Mateo, CA, is the first network that combines recruiting, career development and hiring management services to serve employers and employees at every step. Through its units BrassRing.com and HireSystems, BrassRing provides an array of on- and off-line resources that help employers simplify and accelerate the hiring process, and help individuals to build skills and find a better job. Kaplan is BrassRing's majority shareholder.